VISUAL
ELEMENTS 3

D0841306

VISUAL ELEMENTS

All of the material in the **Visual Elements** series is copyright free and has been expressly created for advertising, publishing, printing and visual communications applications.

The 120 plus pages and more than 400 high quality illustrations are camera ready to be photocopied or photostated and clipped and pasted. The illustrations are printed on only one side so they *can* be clipped right from the book.

Visual Elements 1: Pictograms is a comprehensive volume containing more than 400 pieces of high-quality clip art, featuring pictograms and images of sports, business, recreation and nature.

Visual Elements 2: Sports includes over 600 original line drawn sports illustrations from sailing to sumo wrestling and suitable for use in an unlimited number of graphics applications.

Visual Elements 3: Marks and Patterns, available in late 1989, offers a dizzying selection of repeating and decorative marks and patterns indispensable to designers, graphics artists or anyone interested in design.

Visual Elements 4: World Folk Patterns contains traditional folk patterns from all over the world: decorative and repeating patterns from China, Egypt, Ireland, Islam, Renaissance Europe, Mexico and the United States.

Visual Elements 5: Animals, available in 1990, is a comprehensive collection of original line drawn animal figures, from birds to bugs to bears.

Visual Elements 6: Japanese Traditional Patterns available in 1991. The Japanese are famous for balance and grace in design. This sixth volume in the **Visual Elements** series covers a wide variety of repetitive and decorative Japanese patterns.

Visual Elements 7: Objects and Gadgets will be available in 1991 and includes everything from typewriters, radios, and video cameras to wrenches, roller skates and wedding rings.

Visual Elements 8: Plants, available in 1992, includes original line drawings of roses, potted palms, giant oaks, banana trees, onions, apples, pears and a multitude more.

Visual Elements 9: Buildings & Vehicles, also available in 1992, offers line drawn illustrations of museums, cathedrals, mosques, stadiums, cottages; cars, trucks, trains, boats, ships and planes.

Visual Elements 10: Human Figures available in 1992. Original high quality line drawings of brides, grooms, warriors, farmers, Africans, Americans, people in ethnic costume, rock stars and children.

VISUAL ELEMENTS 3

MARKS AND PATTERNS
CLIP ART

ROCKPORT PUBLISHERS • ROCKPORT, MASSACHUSETTS
Distributed by North Light Books • Cincinnati, Ohio

Distributed in the U.S. and Canada
by: North Light Books, an
imprint of F & W Publications
1507 Dana Avenue
Cincinnati, Ohio 45207
Telephone: 1-800-289-0963
Fax: 513-531-4744

First published in Great Britain by:
Columbus Books, Ltd.
19-23 Ludgate Hill
London, England EC4M 7PD
Telephone: 01-248-4444
Fax: 01-248-3357
ISBN: 0-86287-528-5

Other distribution by:
Rockport Publishers, Inc.
P.O. Box 396
5 Smith Street
Rockport, Massachusetts 01966
Telephone: 508-546-9590
Telex: 5106019284
Fax: 508-546-7141

First published in Japan.
First English language edition published by
Rockport publishers, Inc.

Printed in the United States

CONTENTS

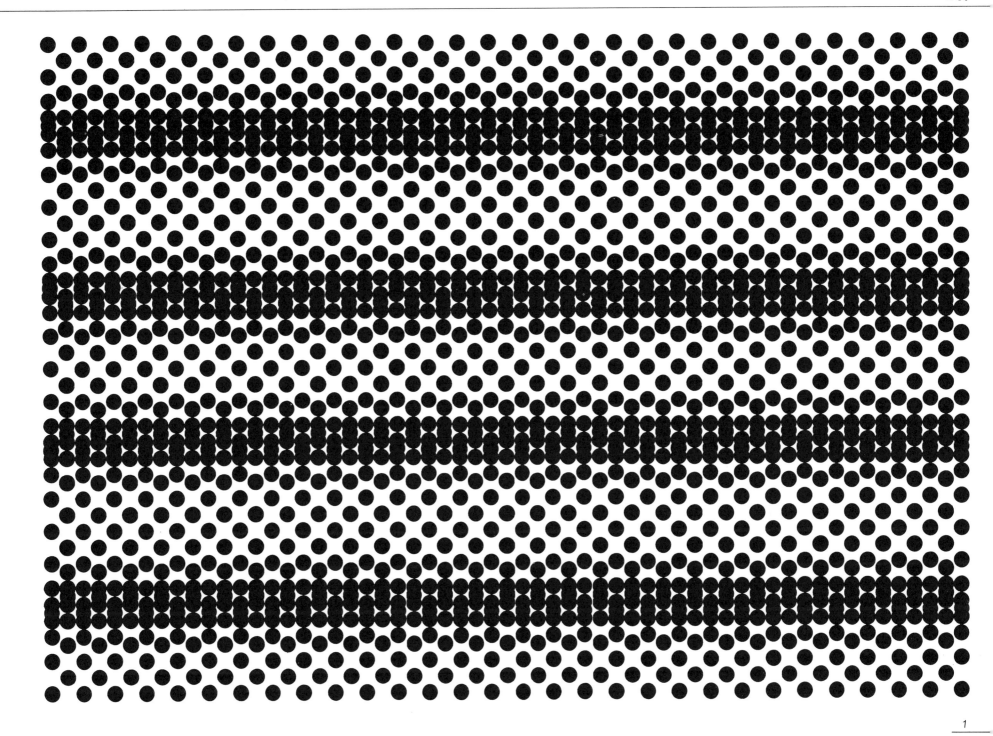

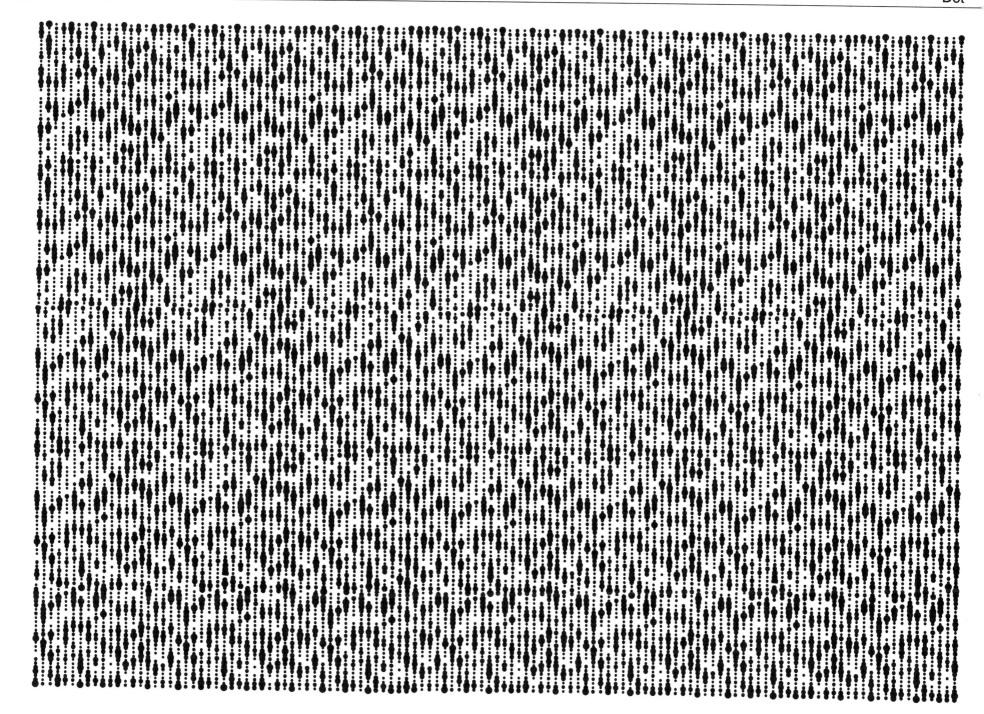

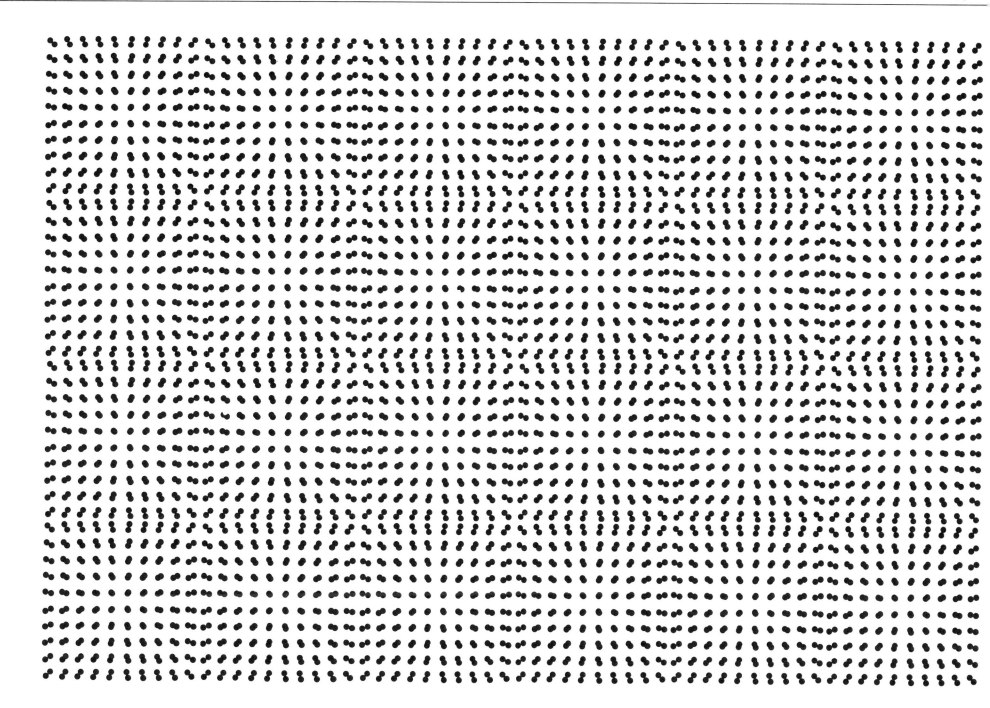

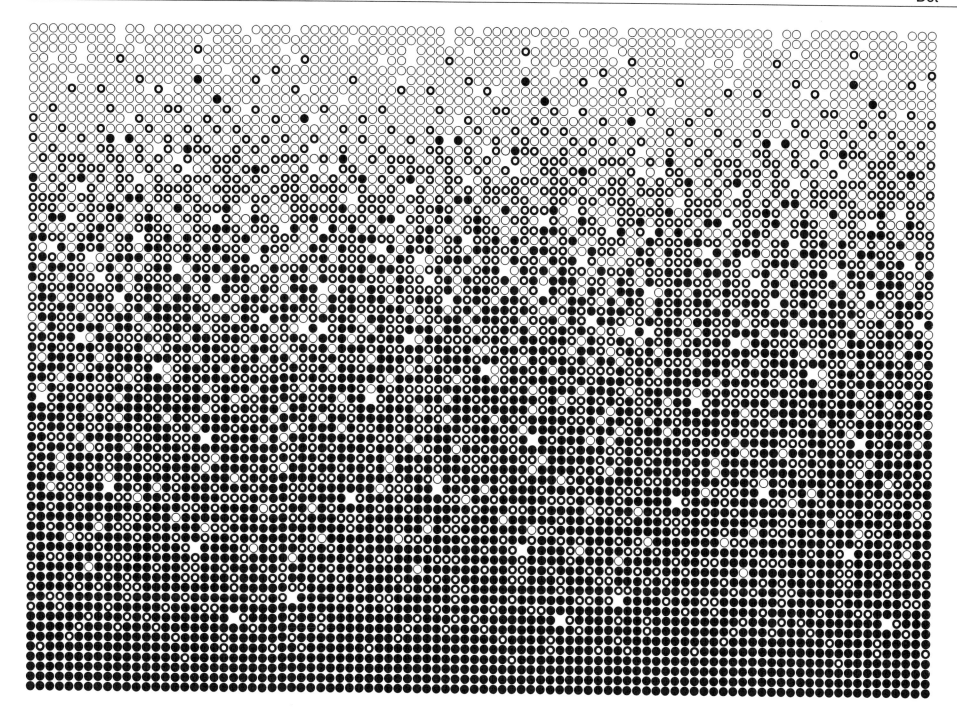

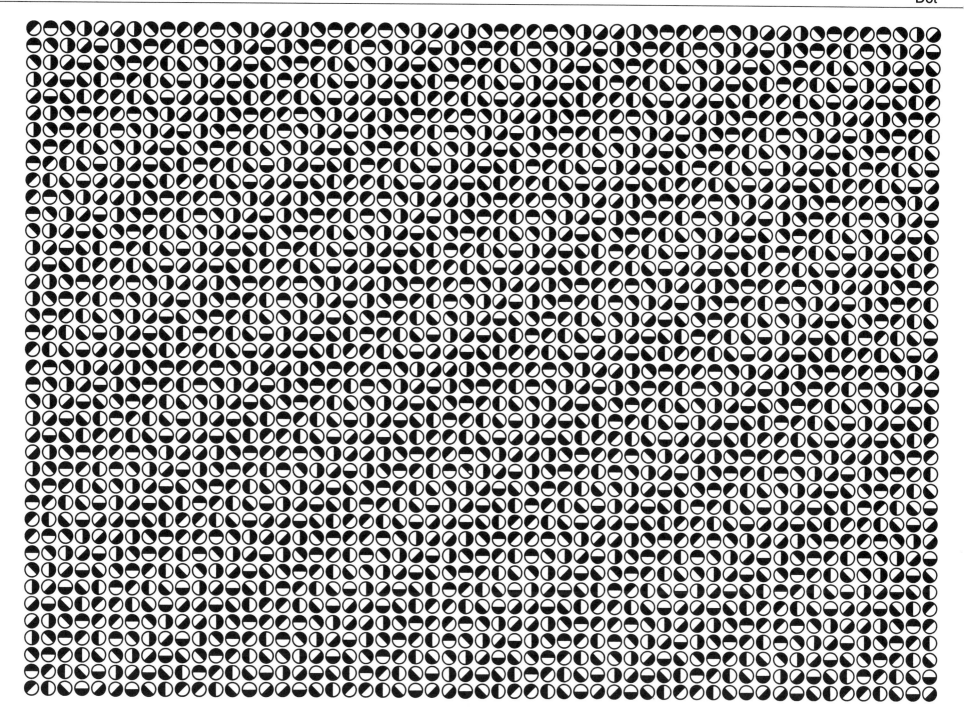

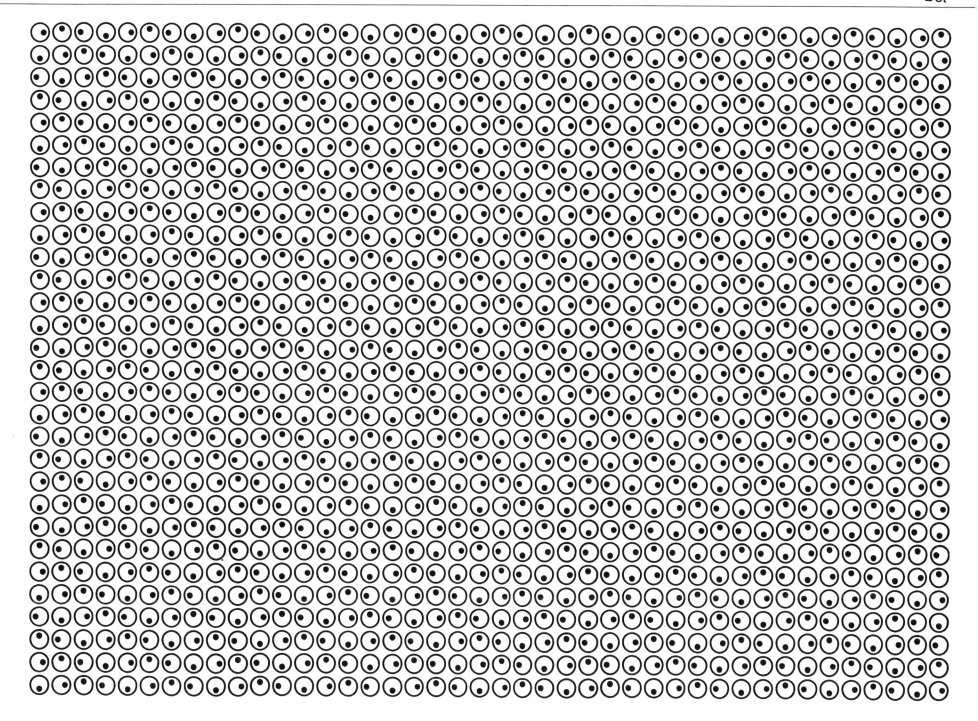

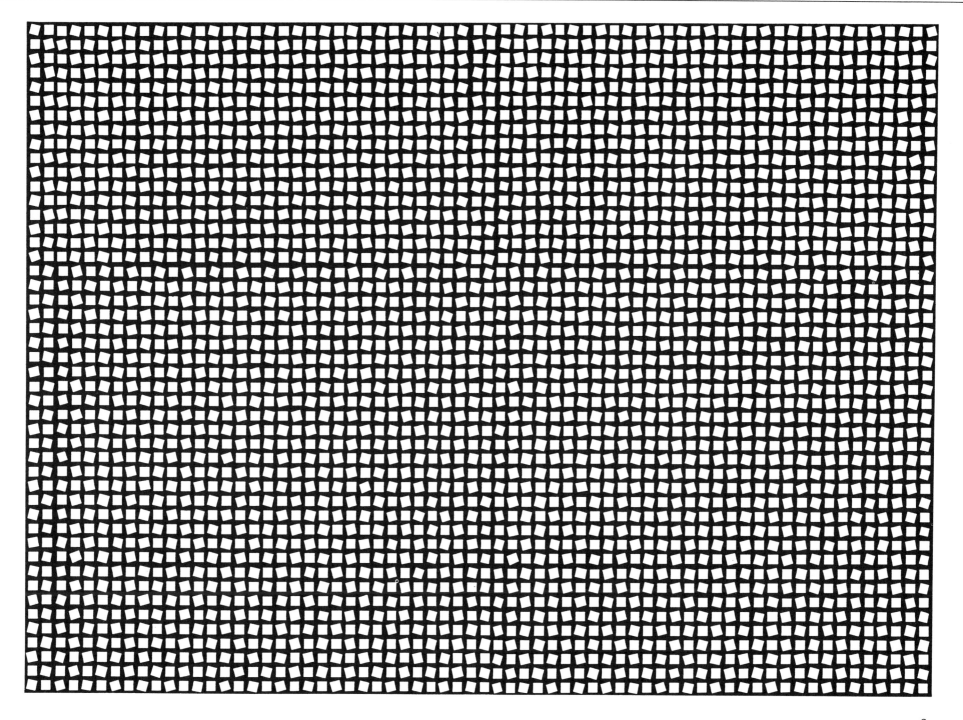

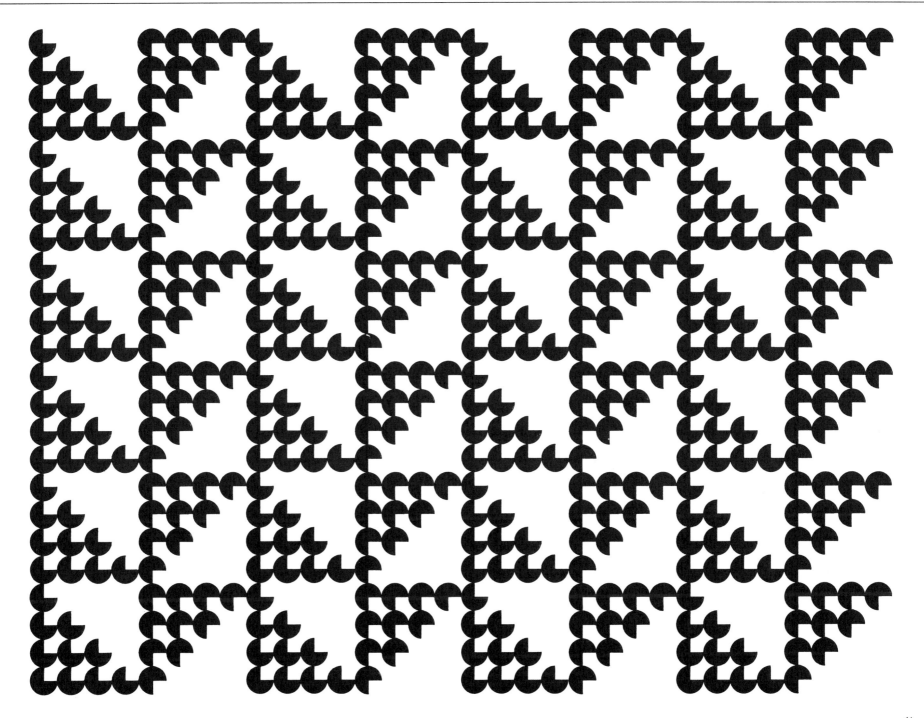

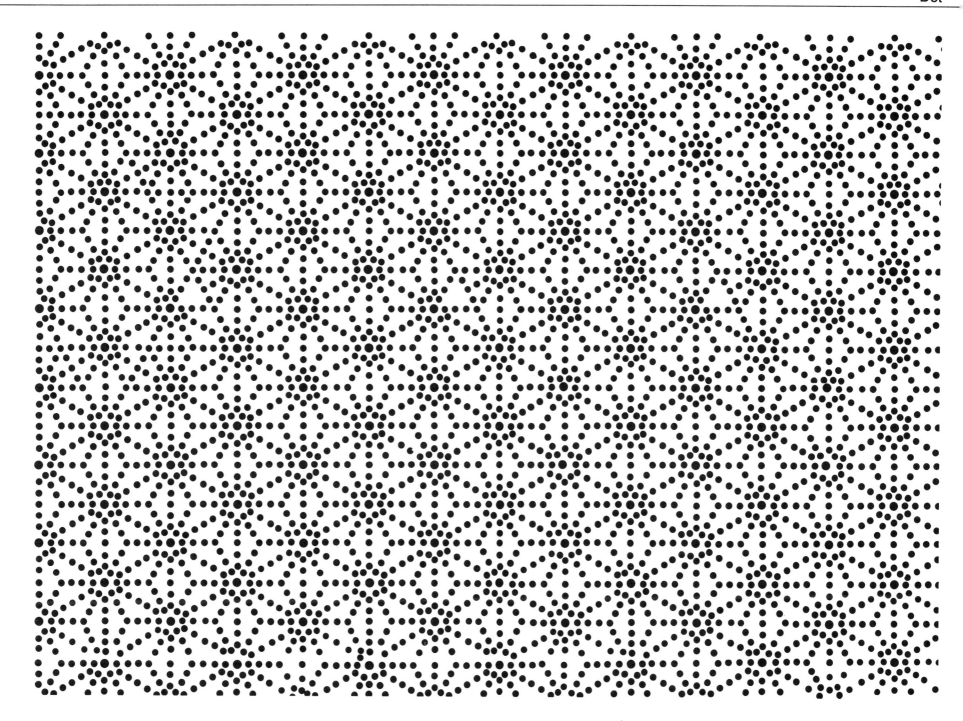

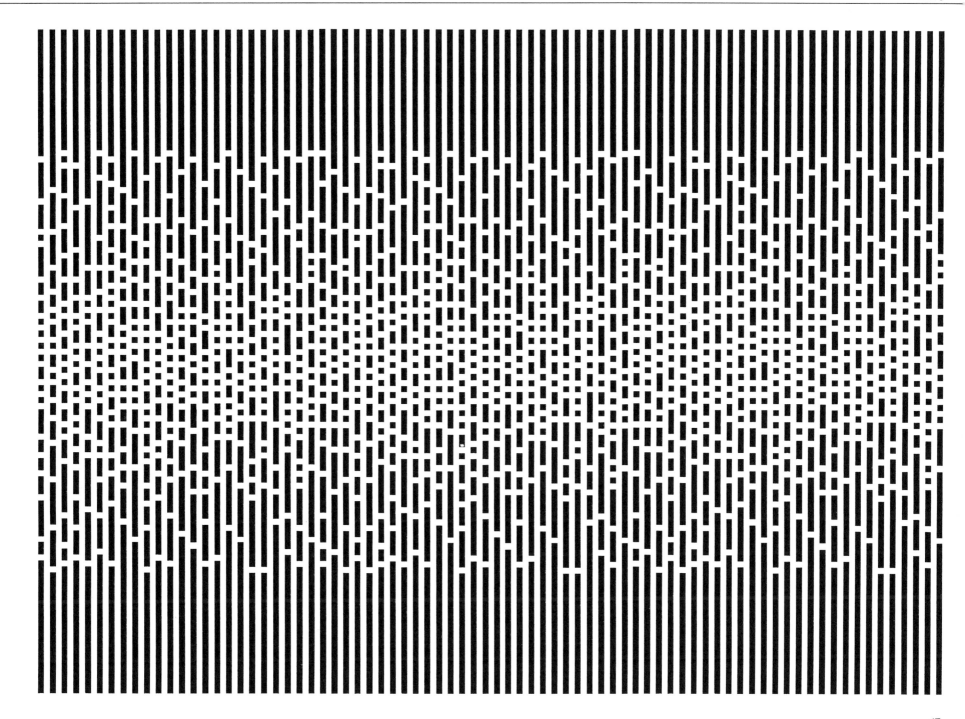

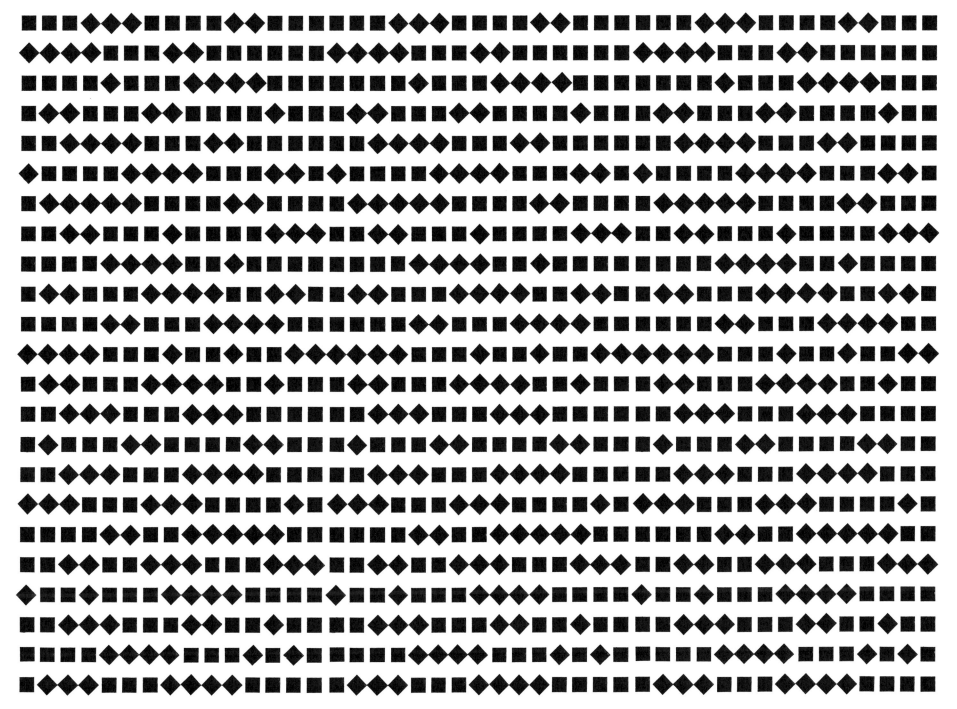

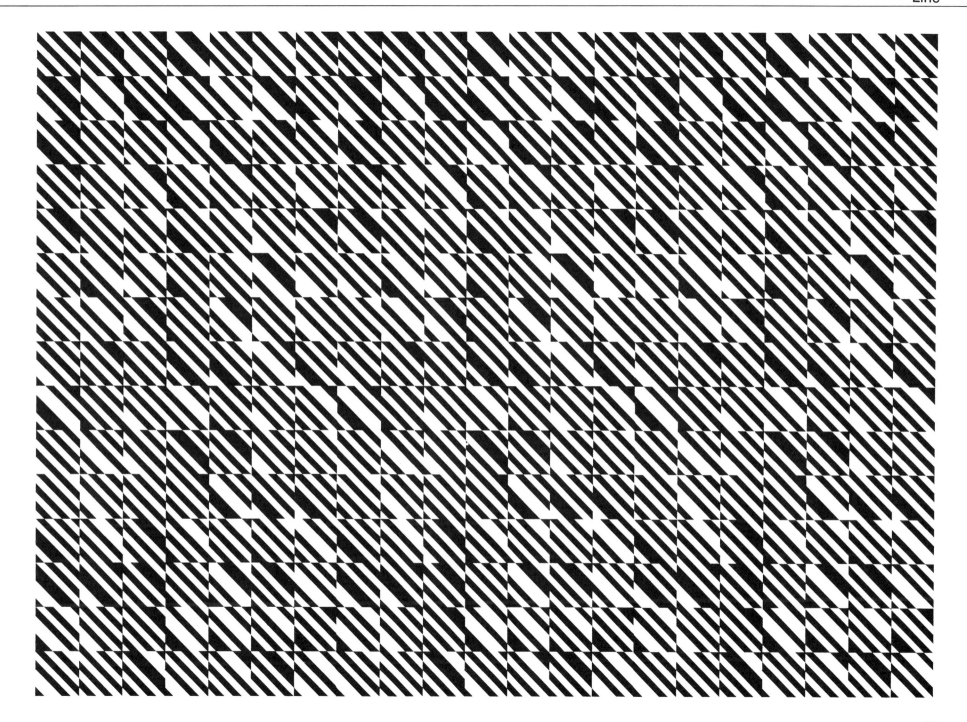

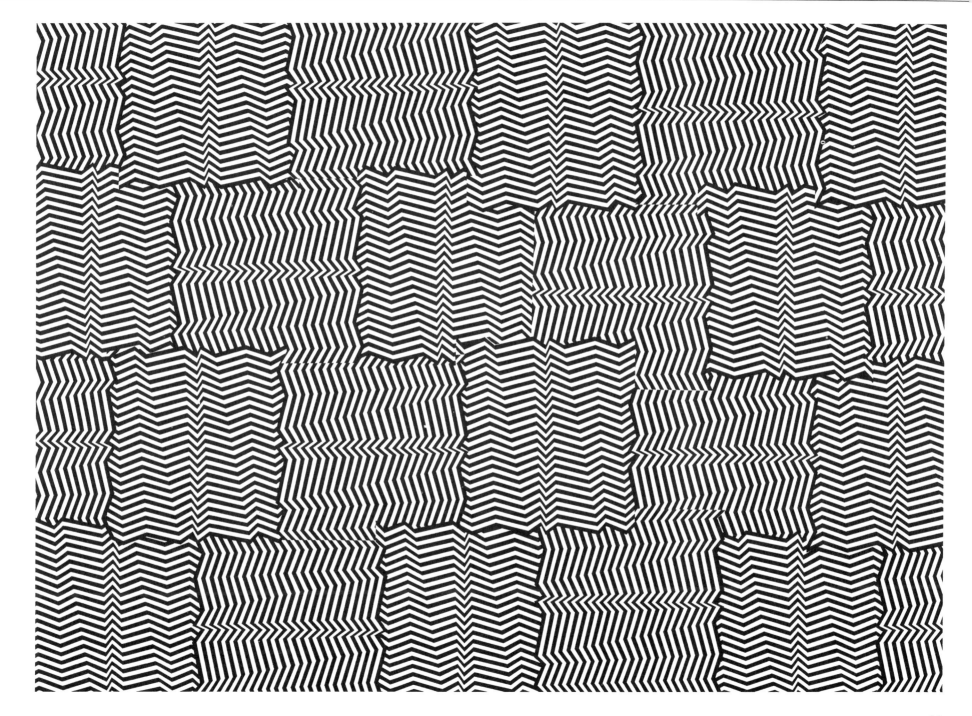

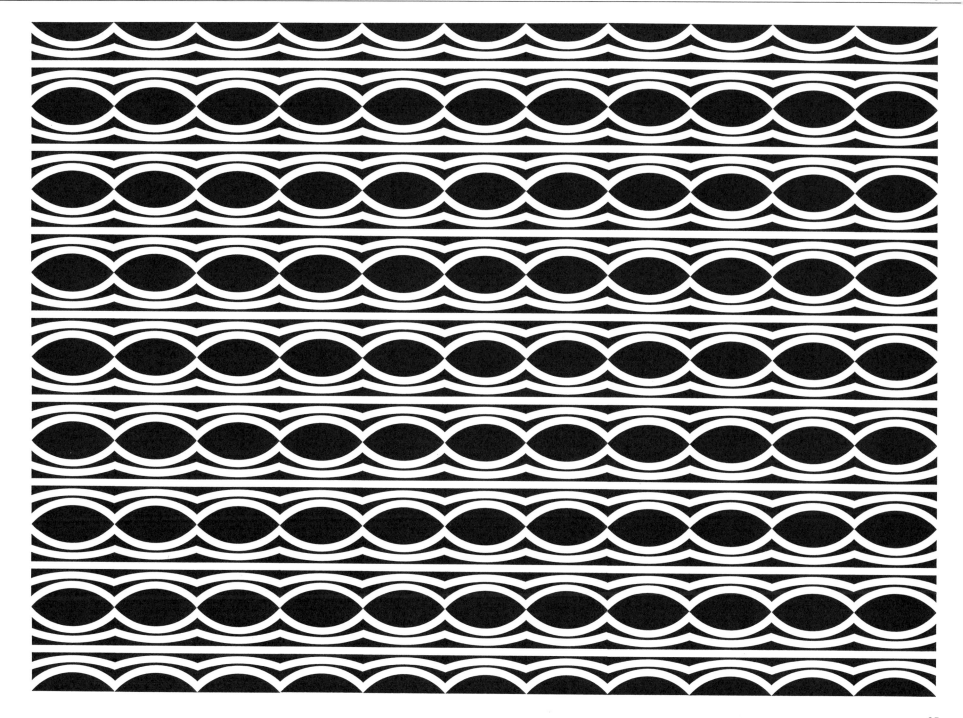

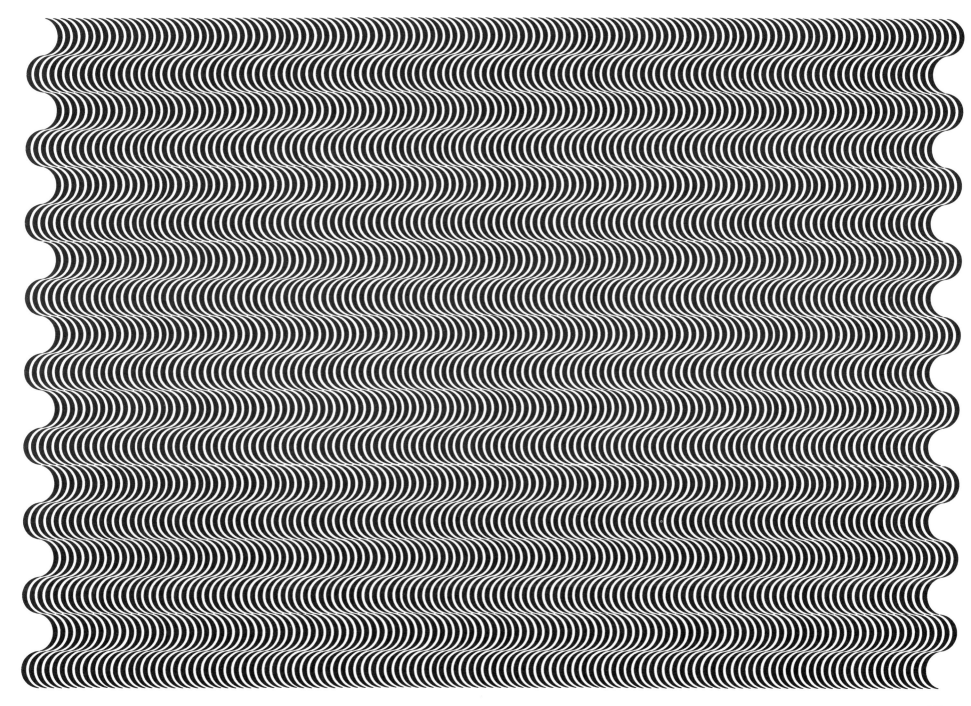

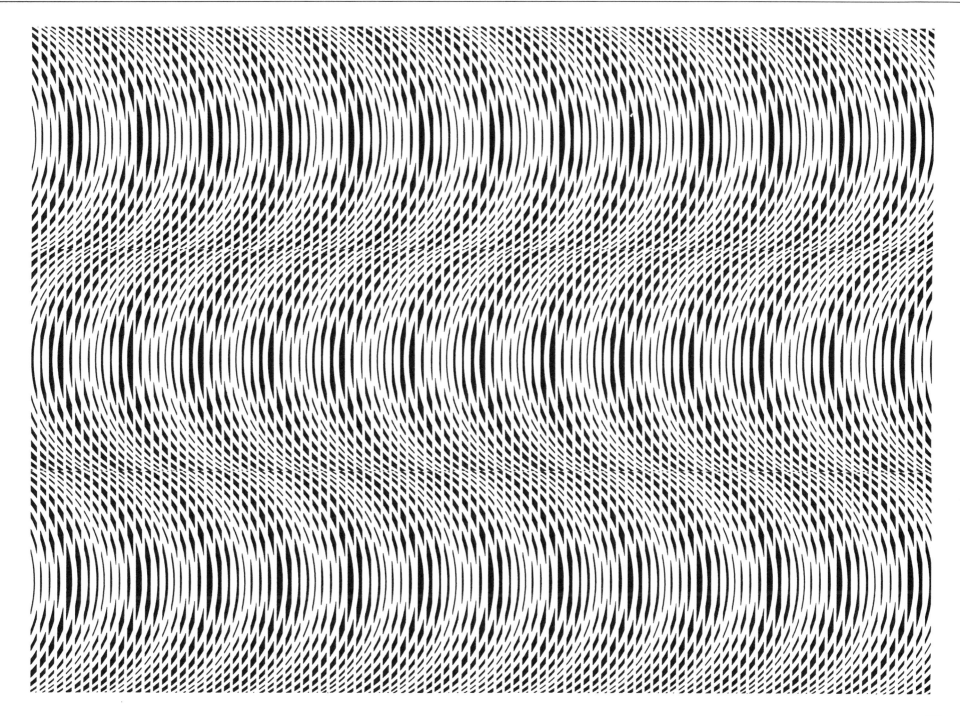

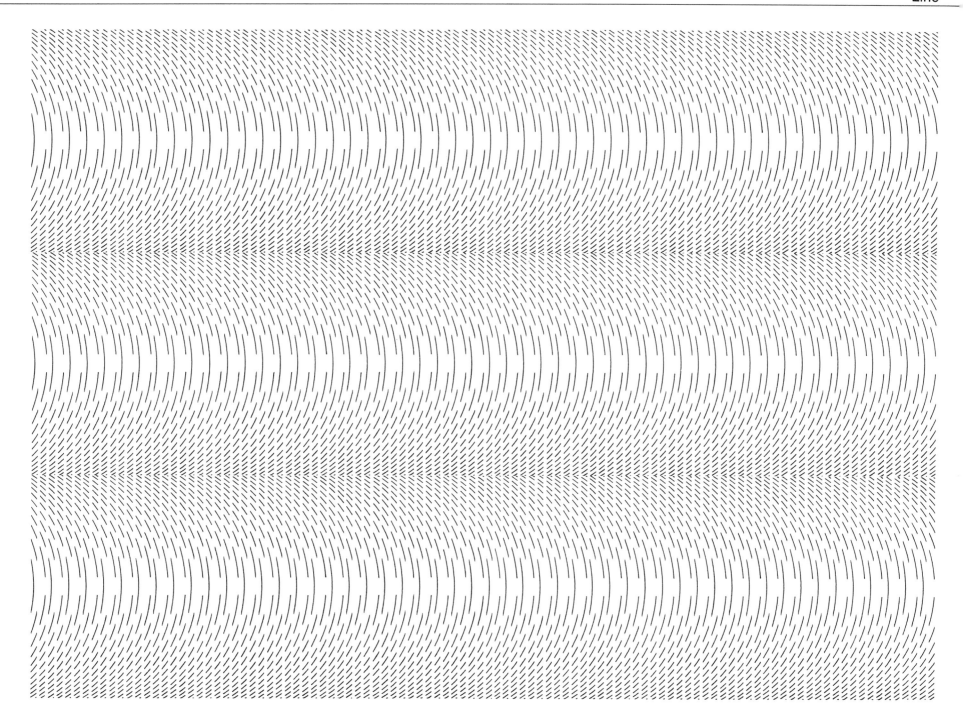

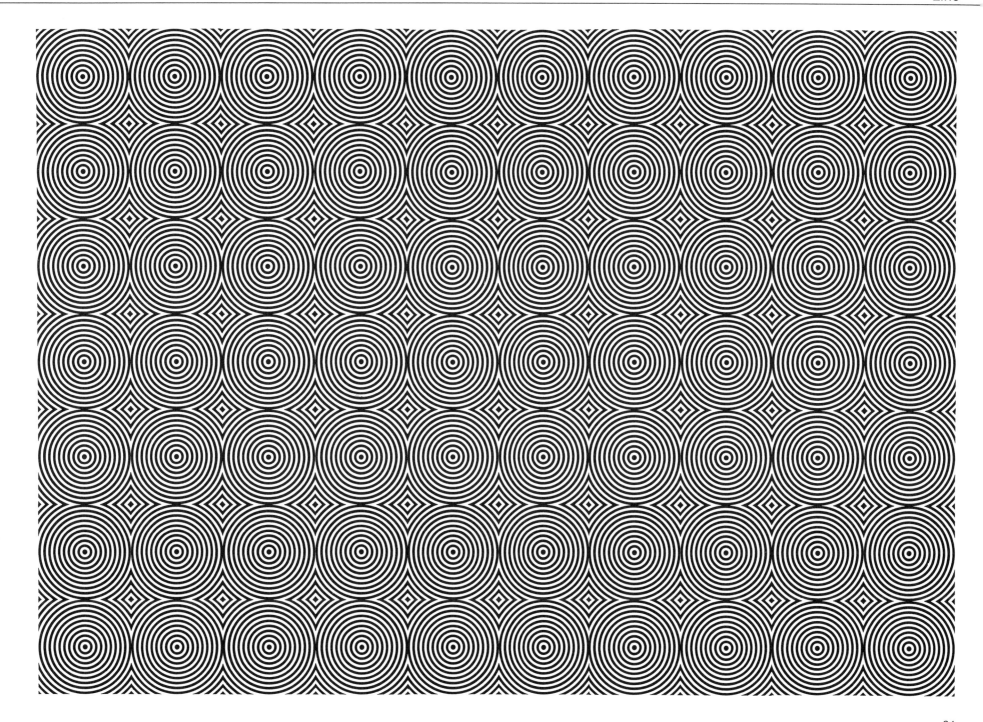

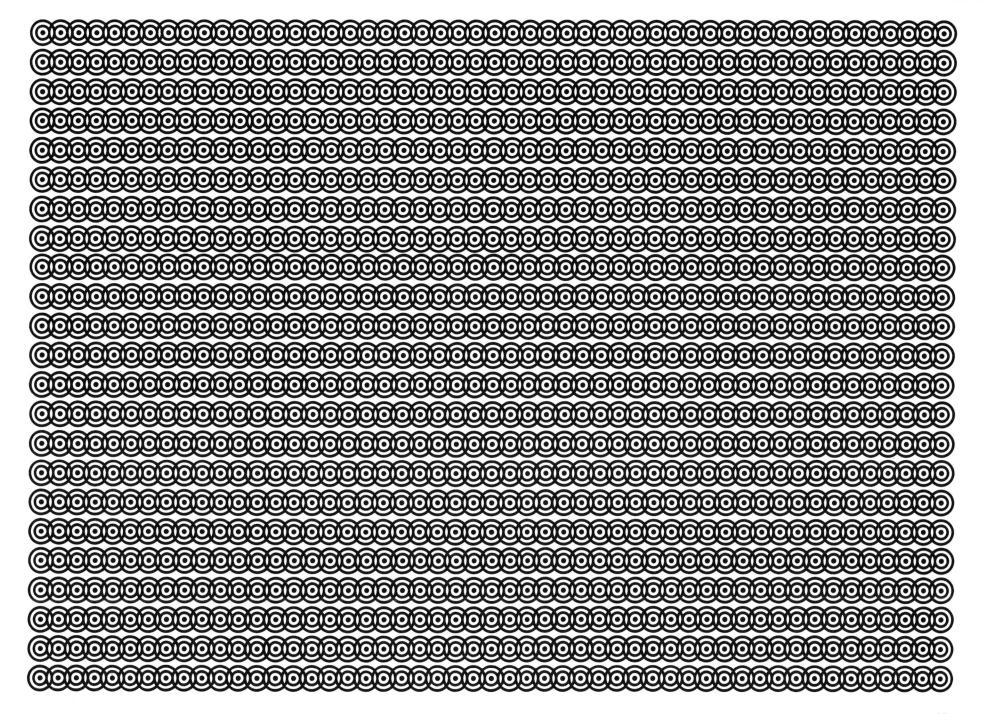

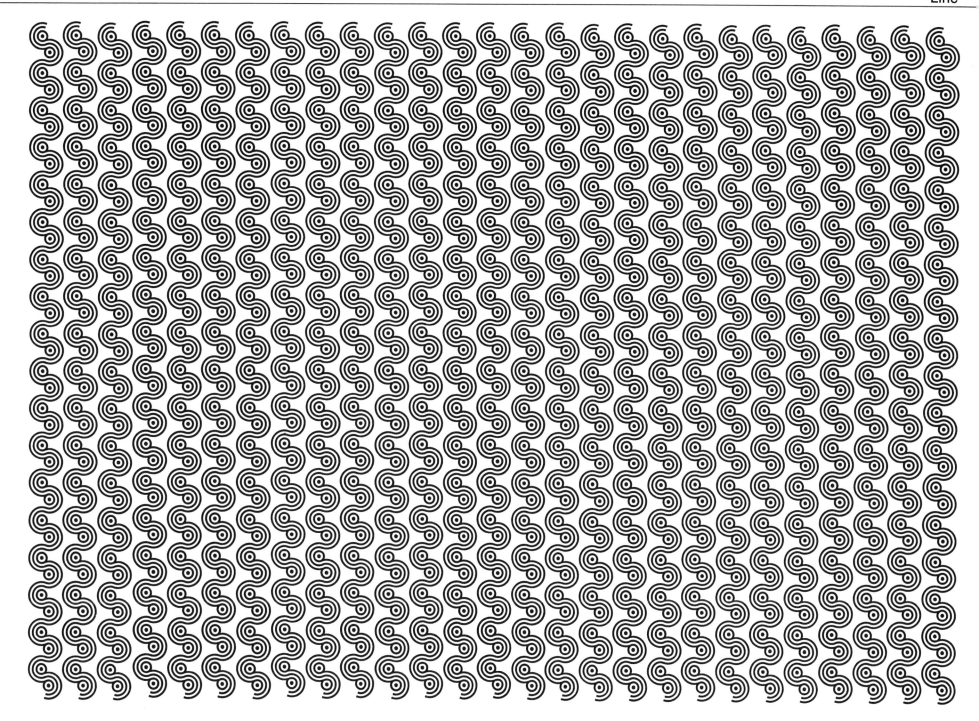

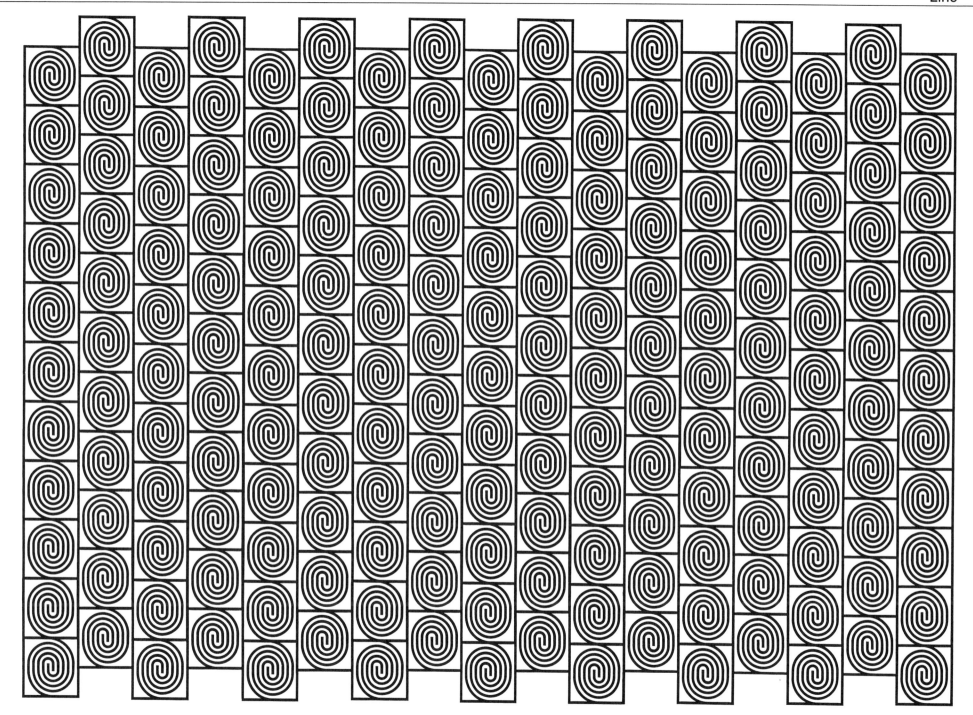

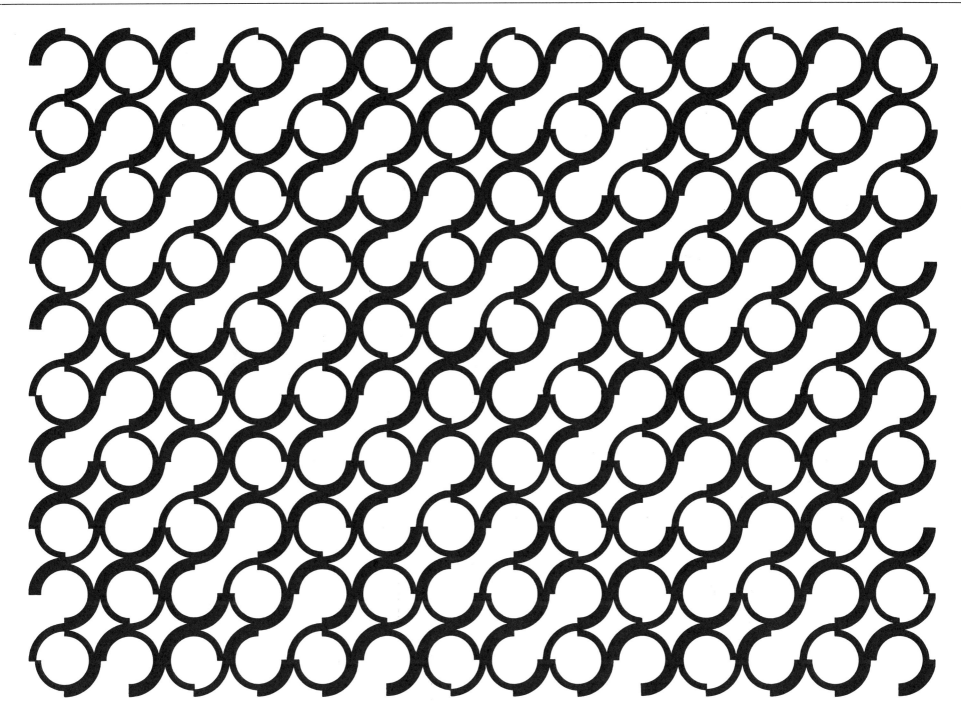

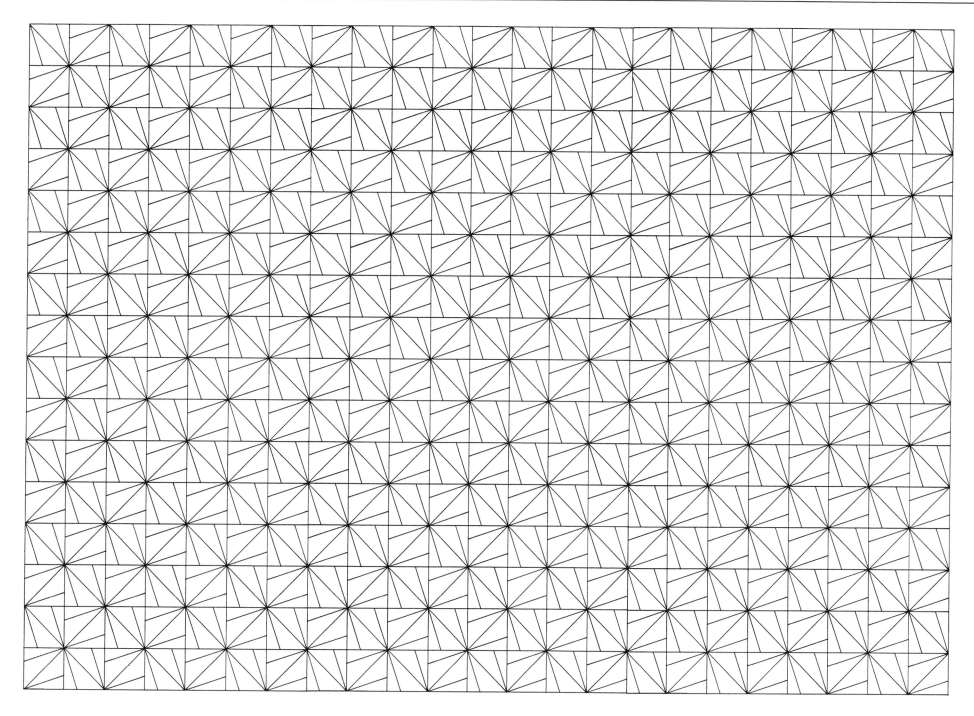

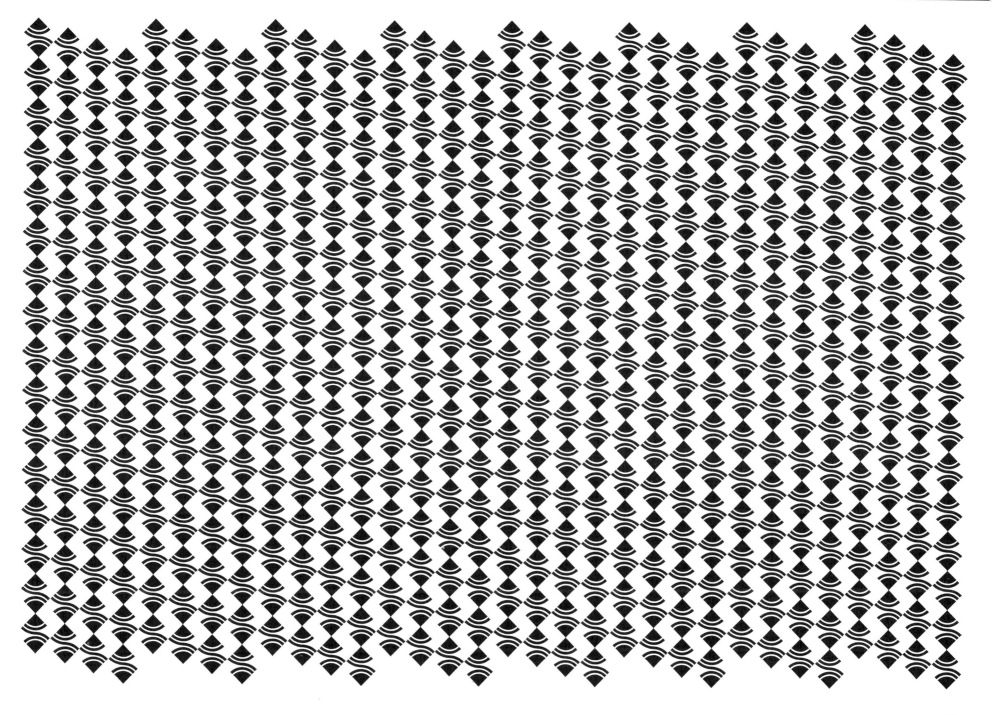

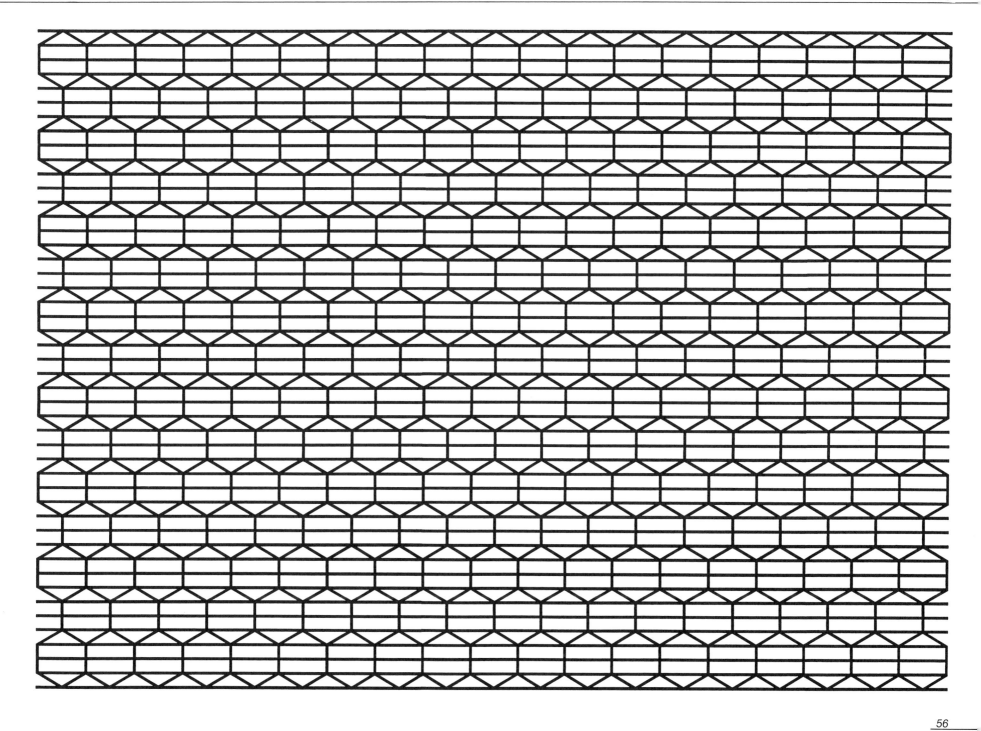

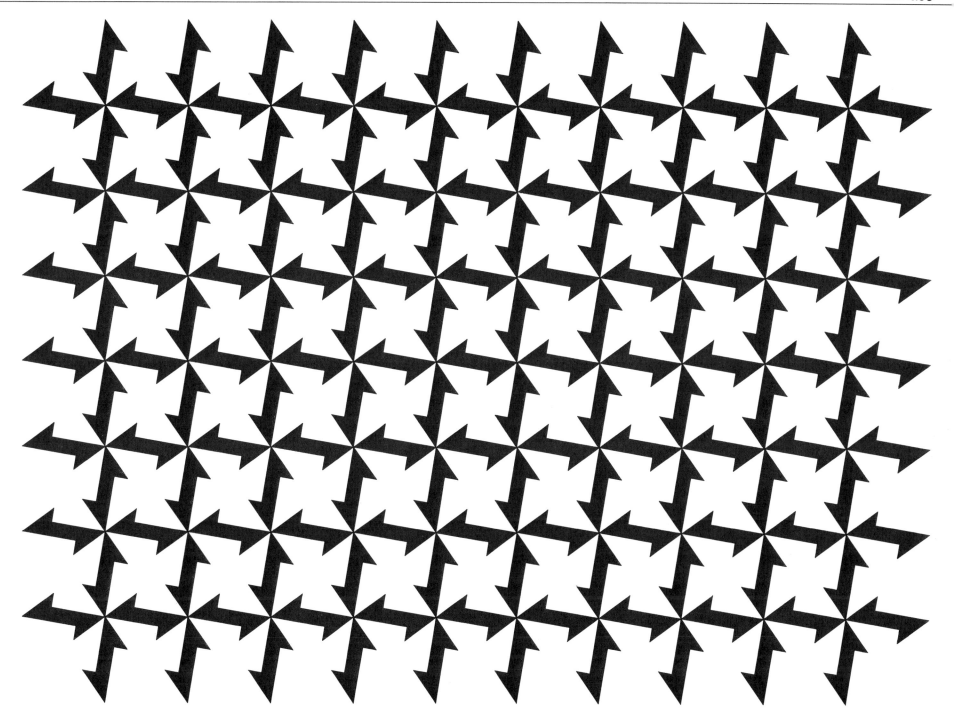

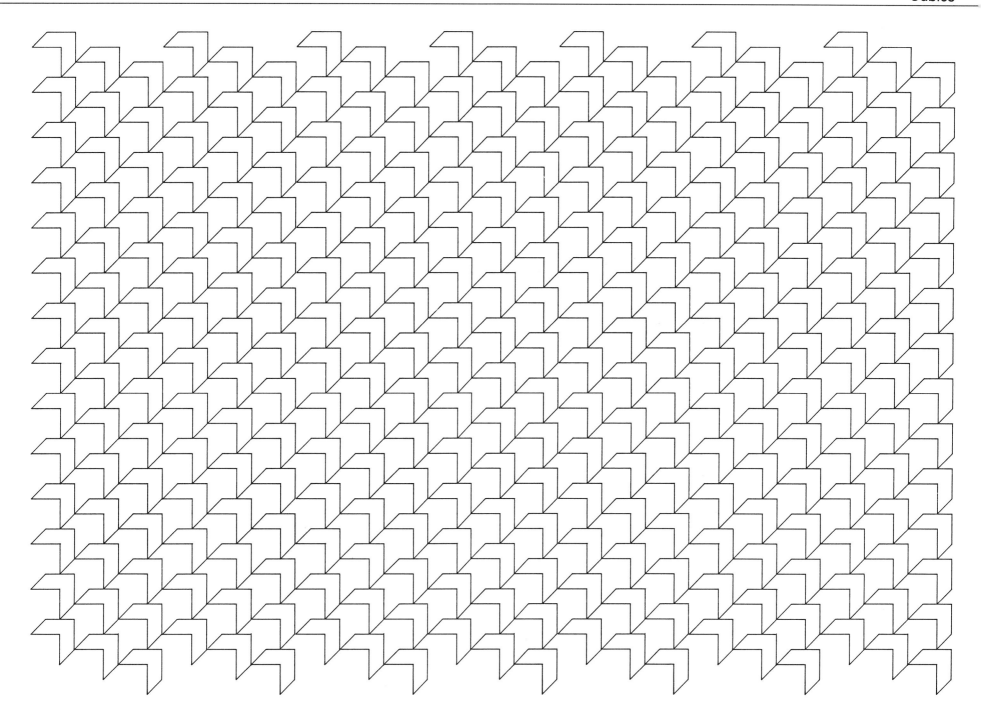

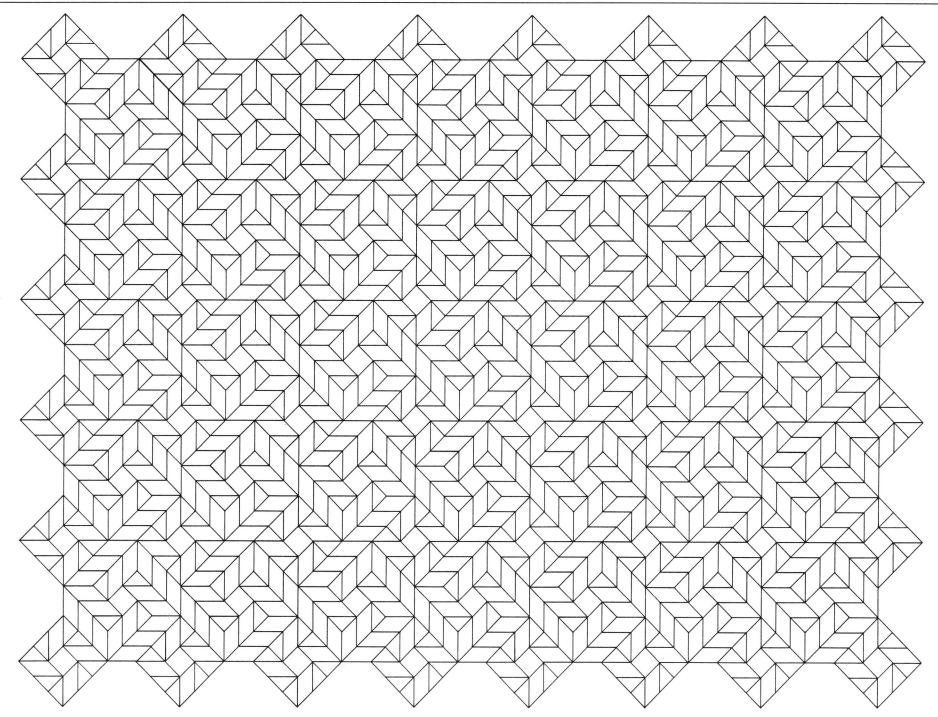

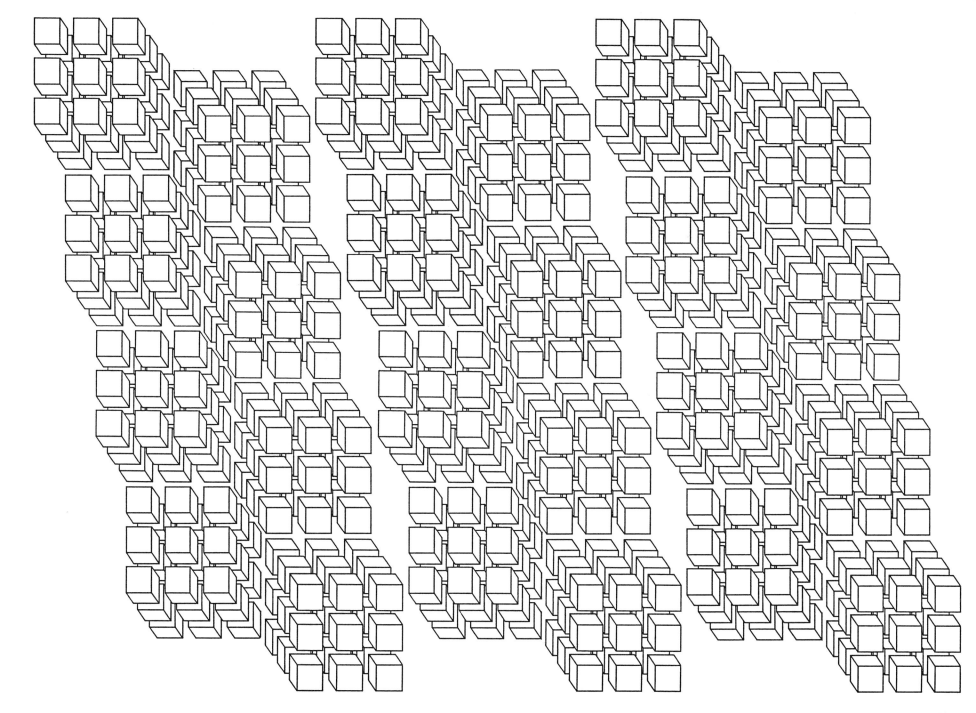

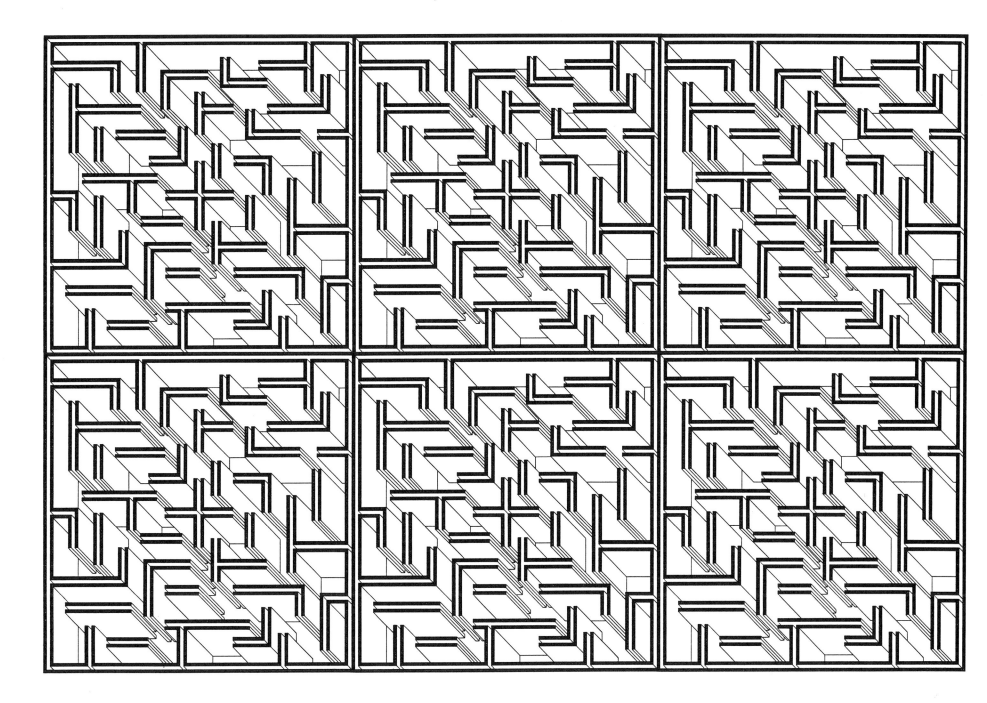

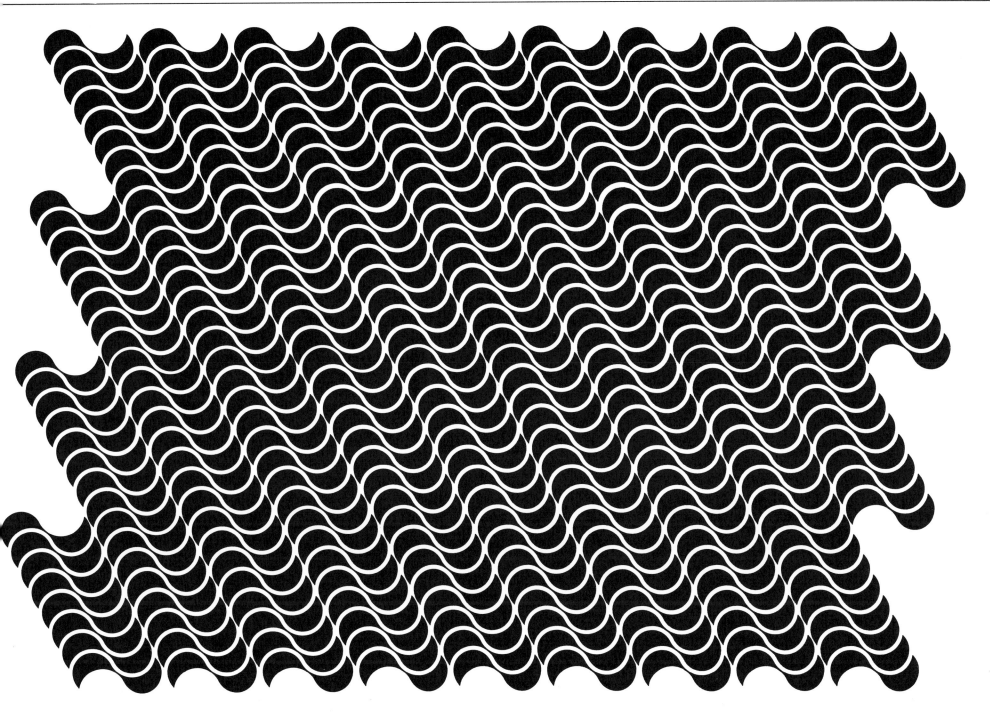

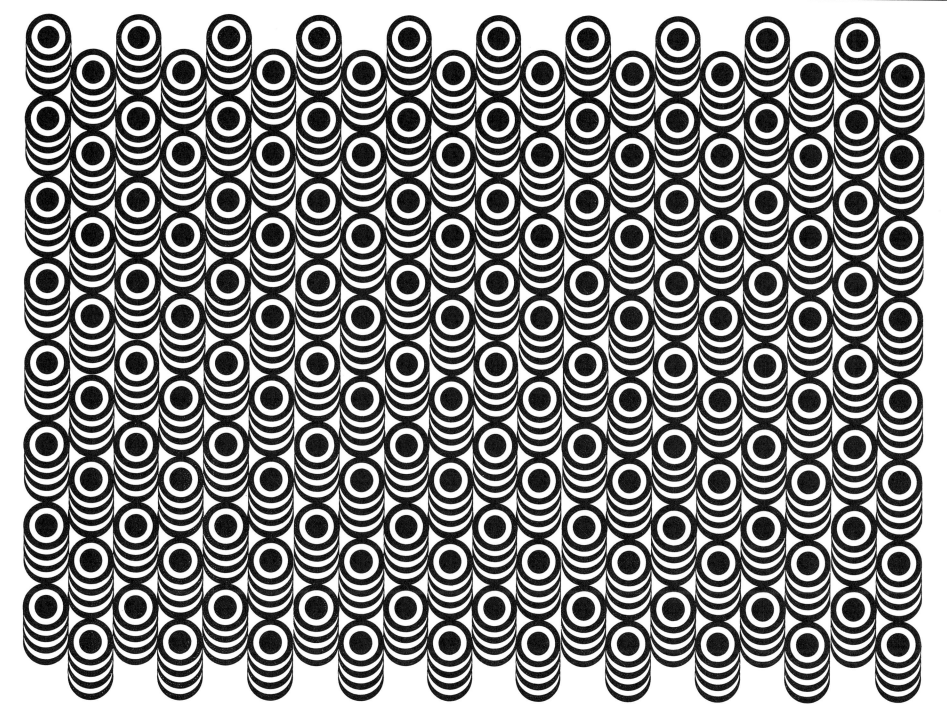

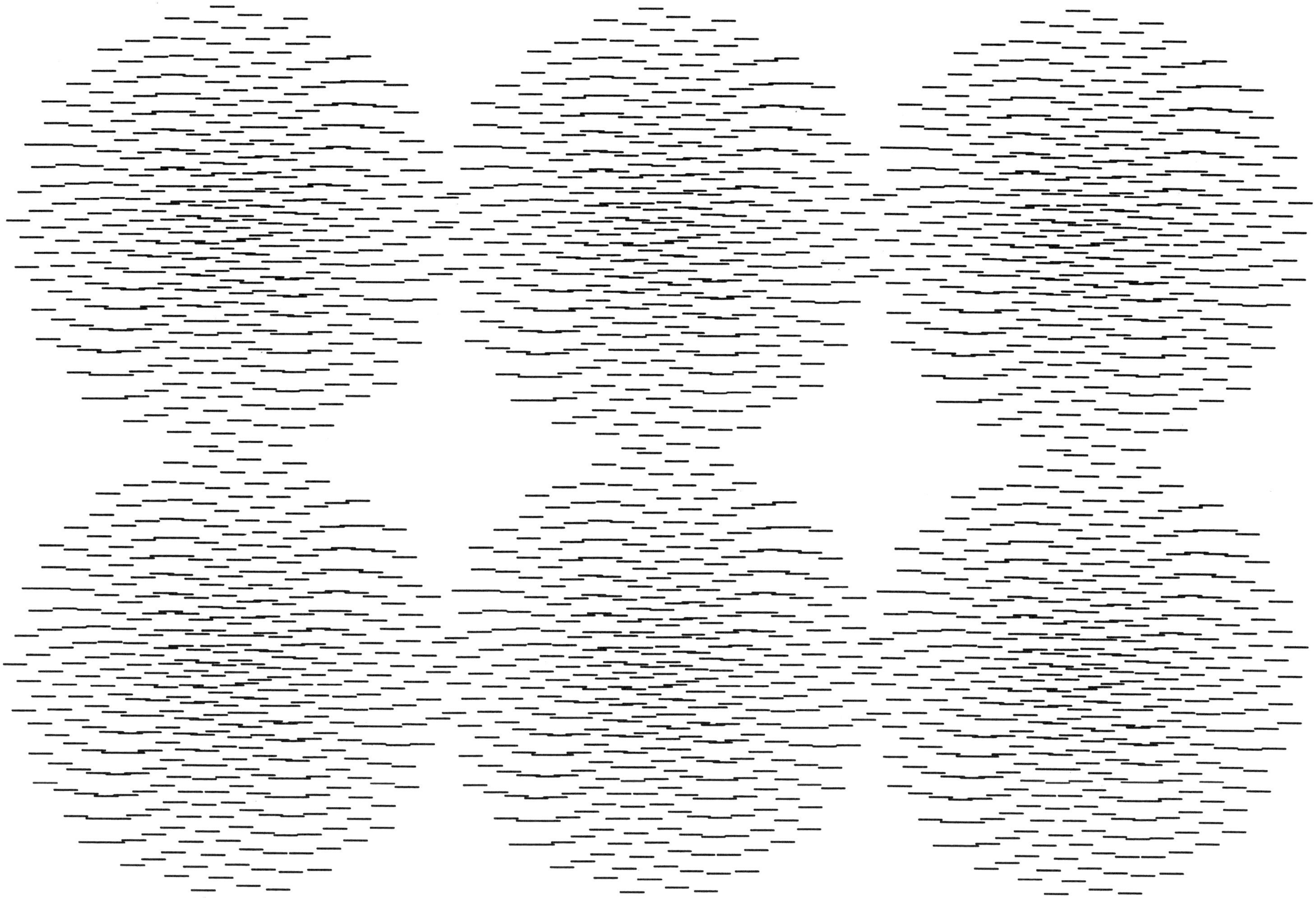

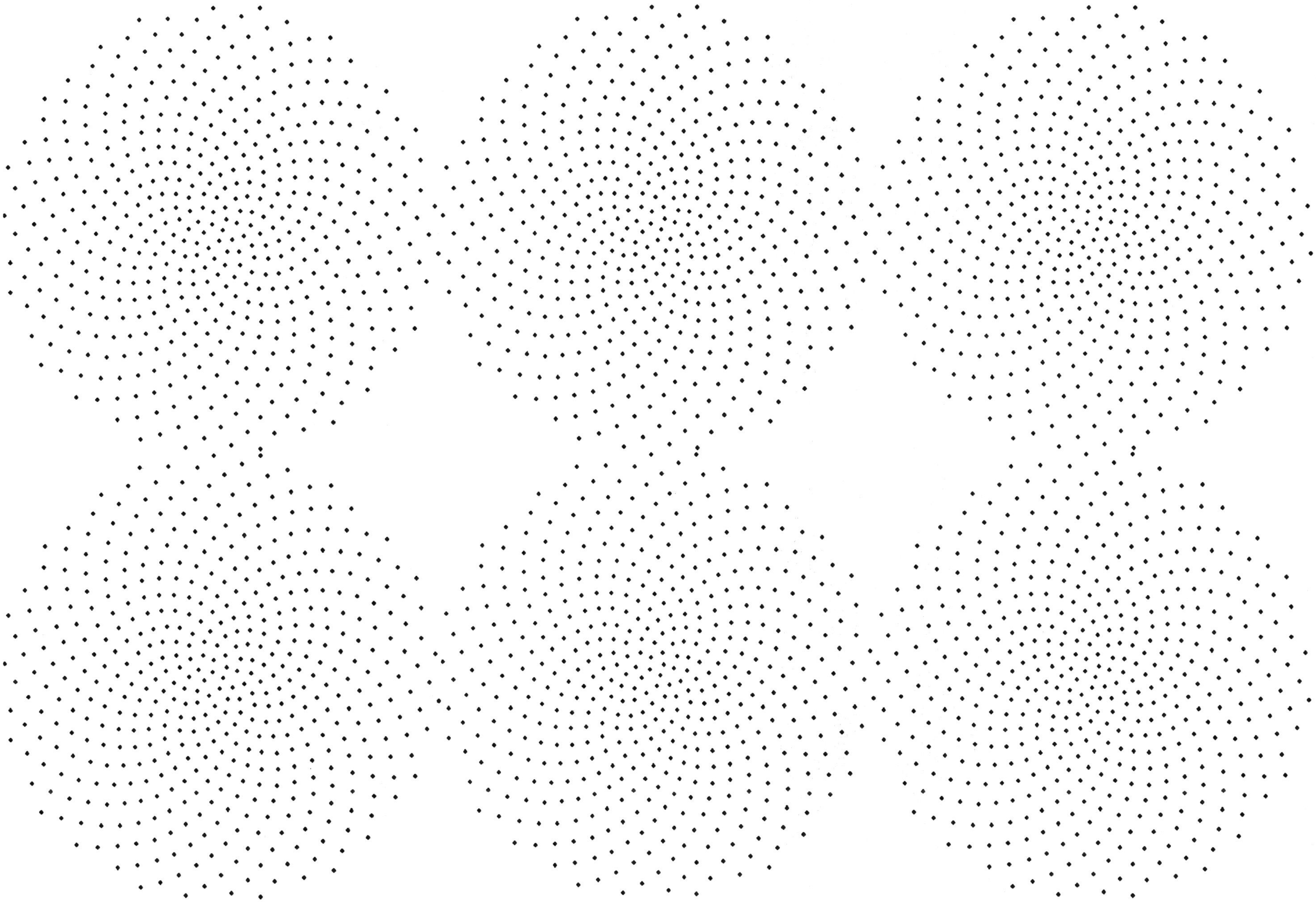

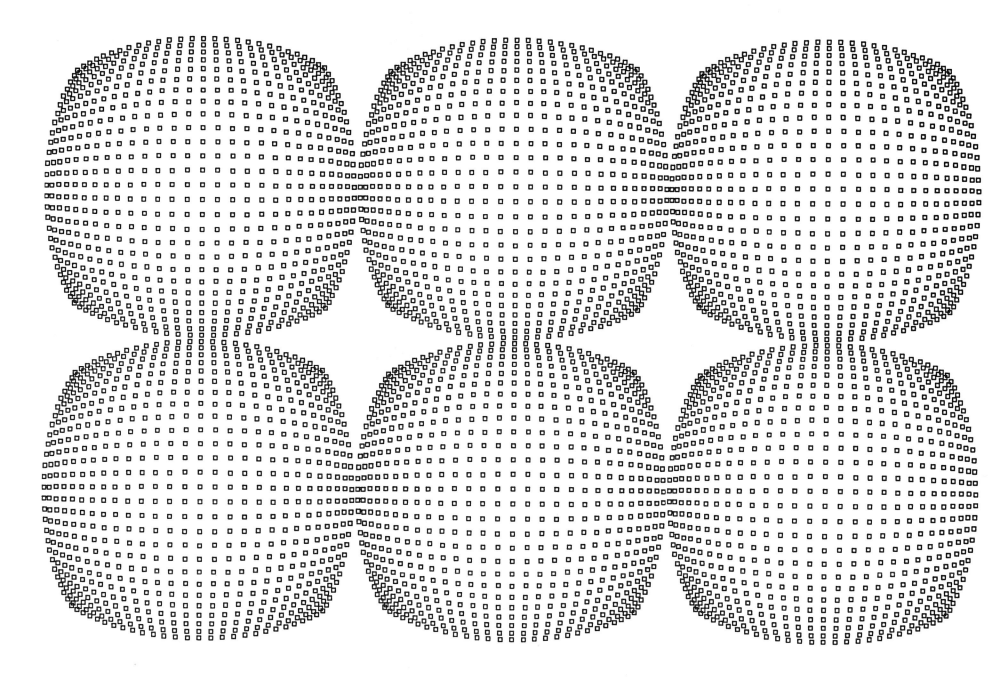

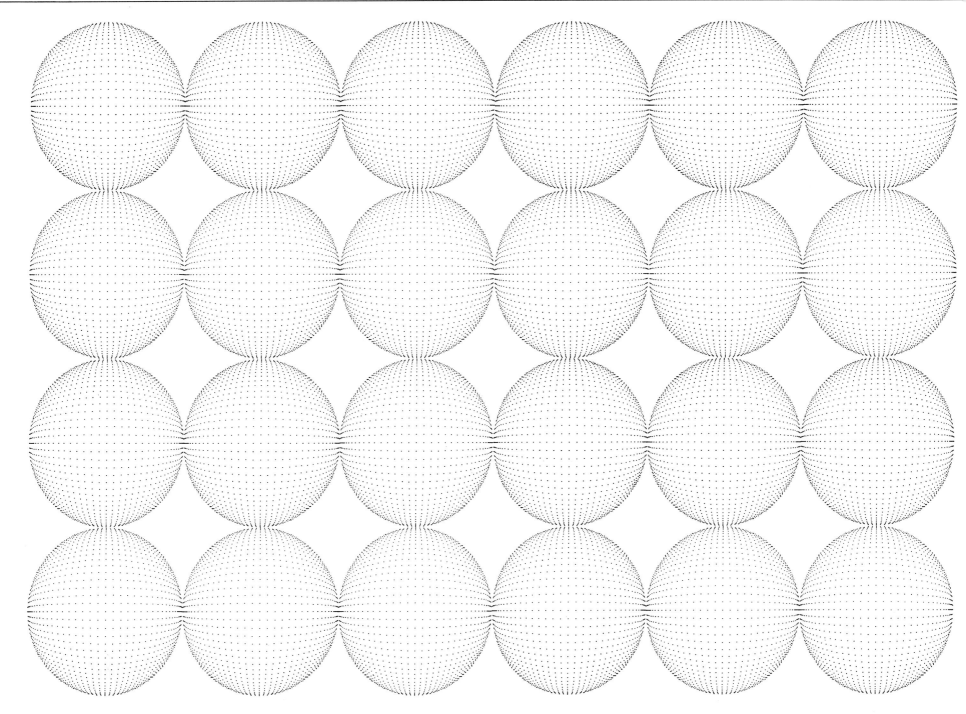

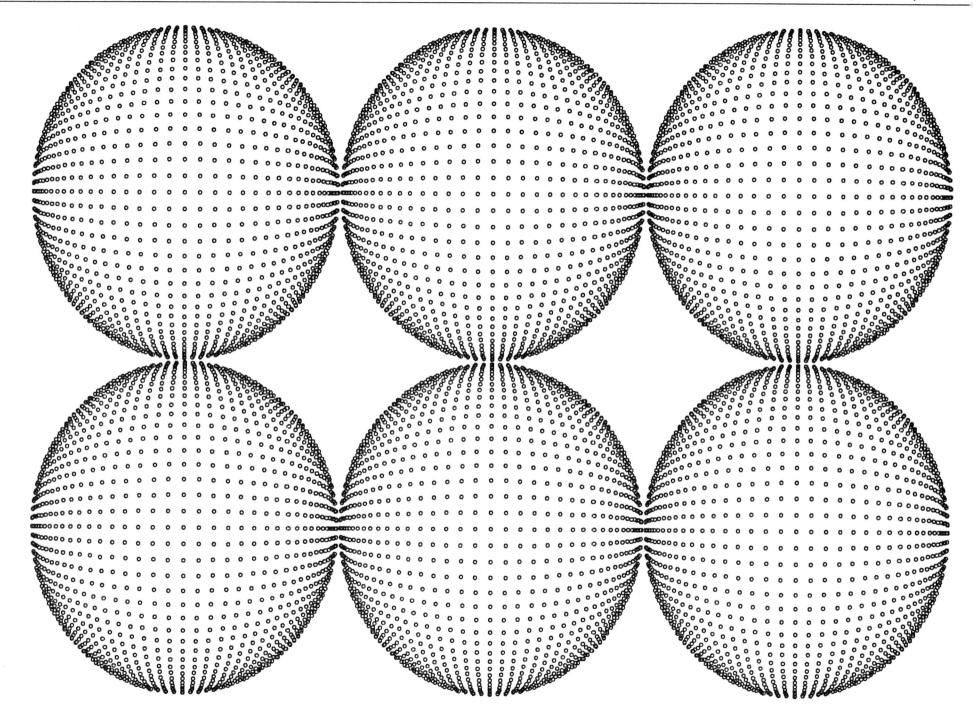

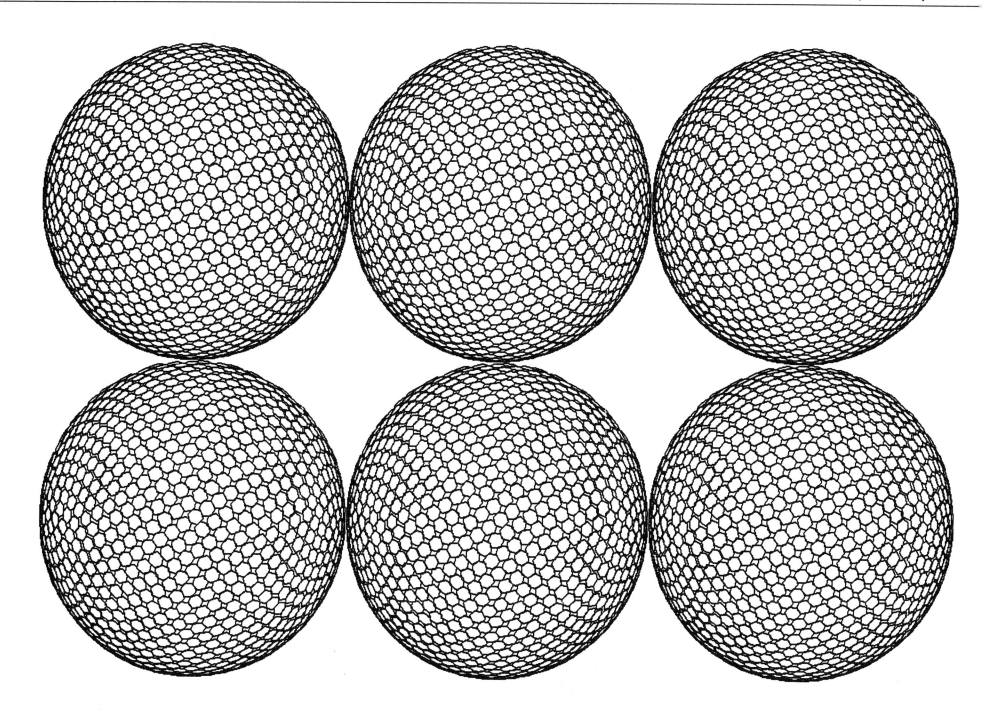

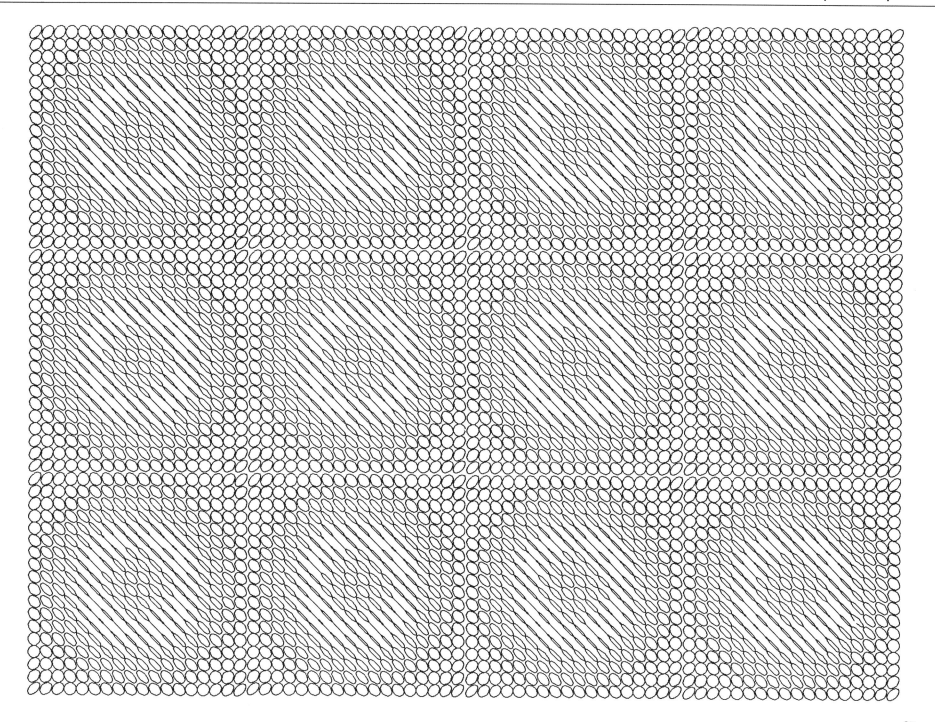

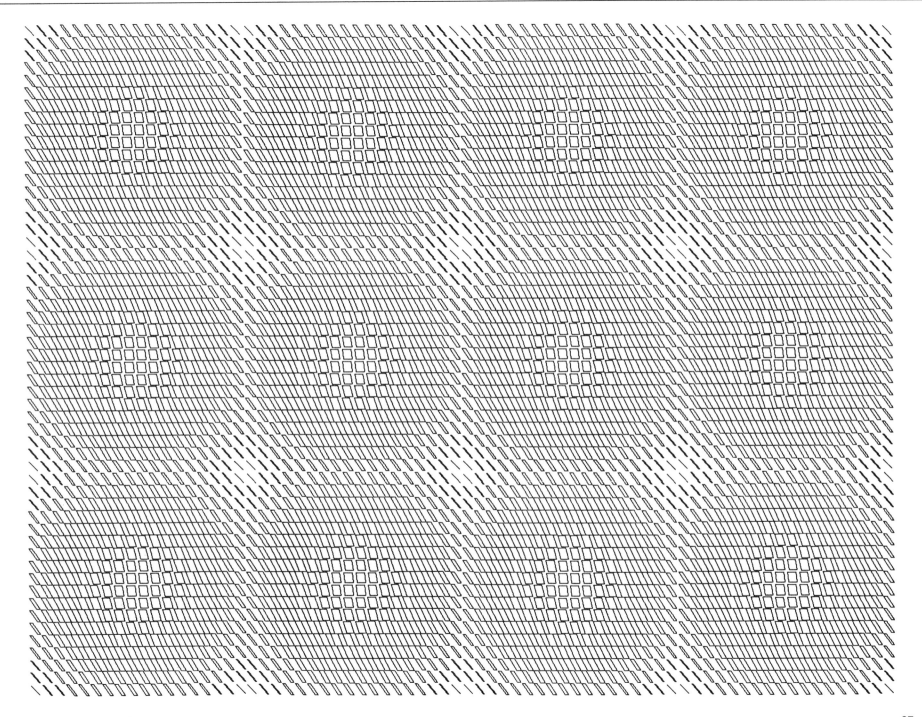

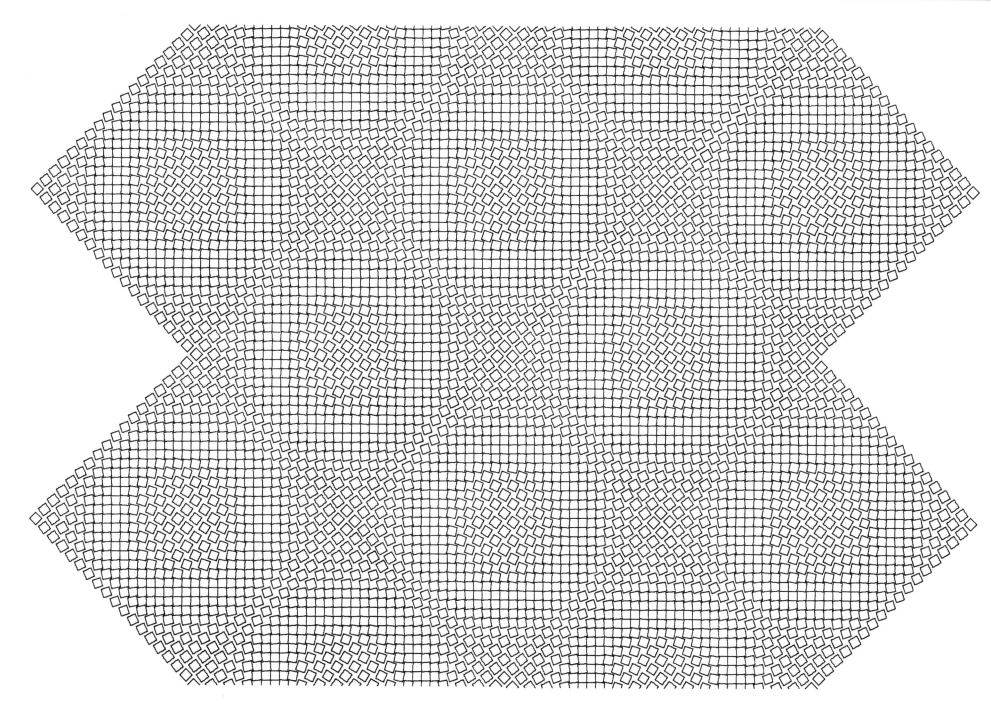

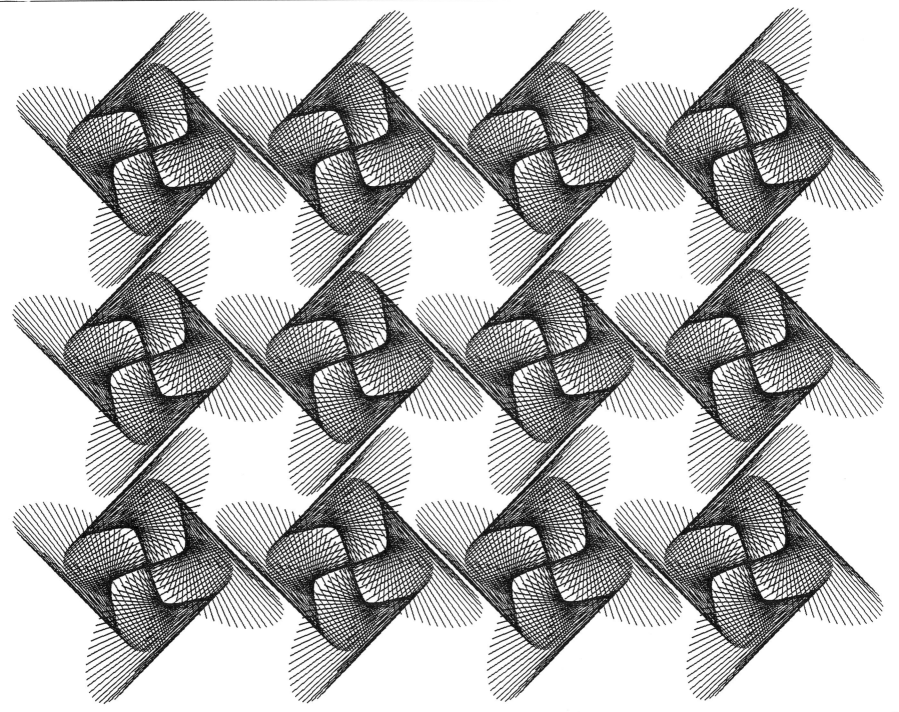

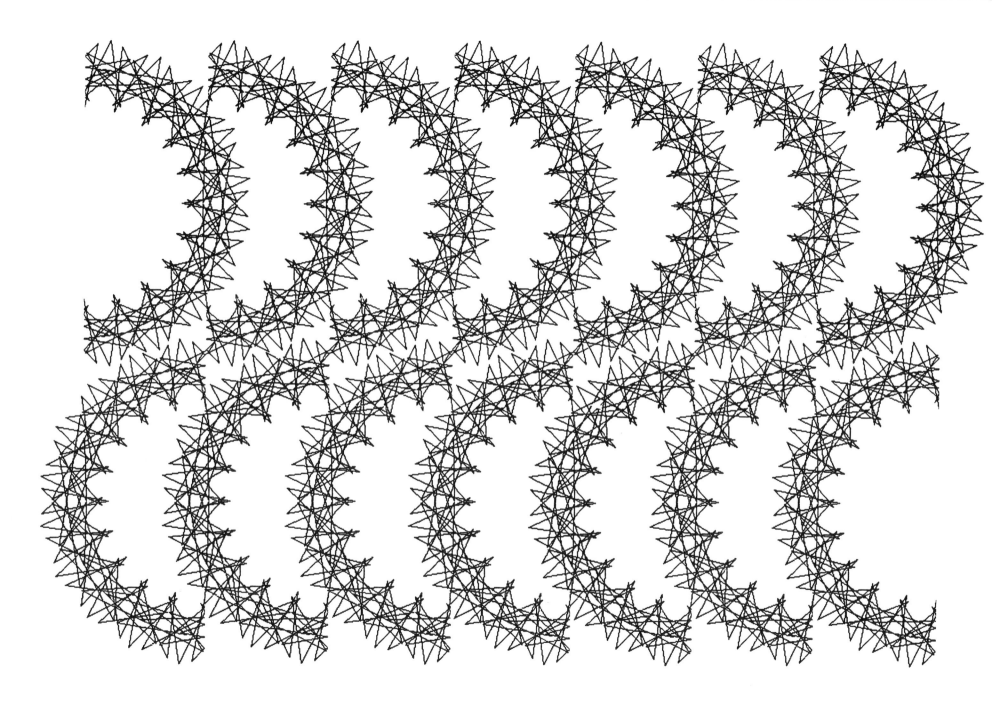

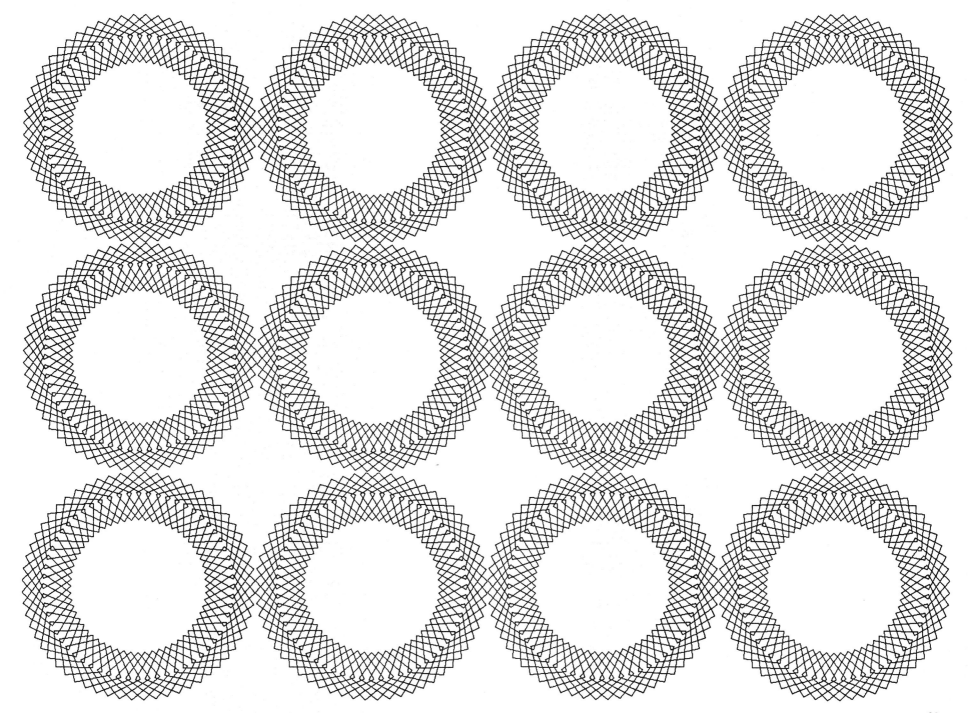

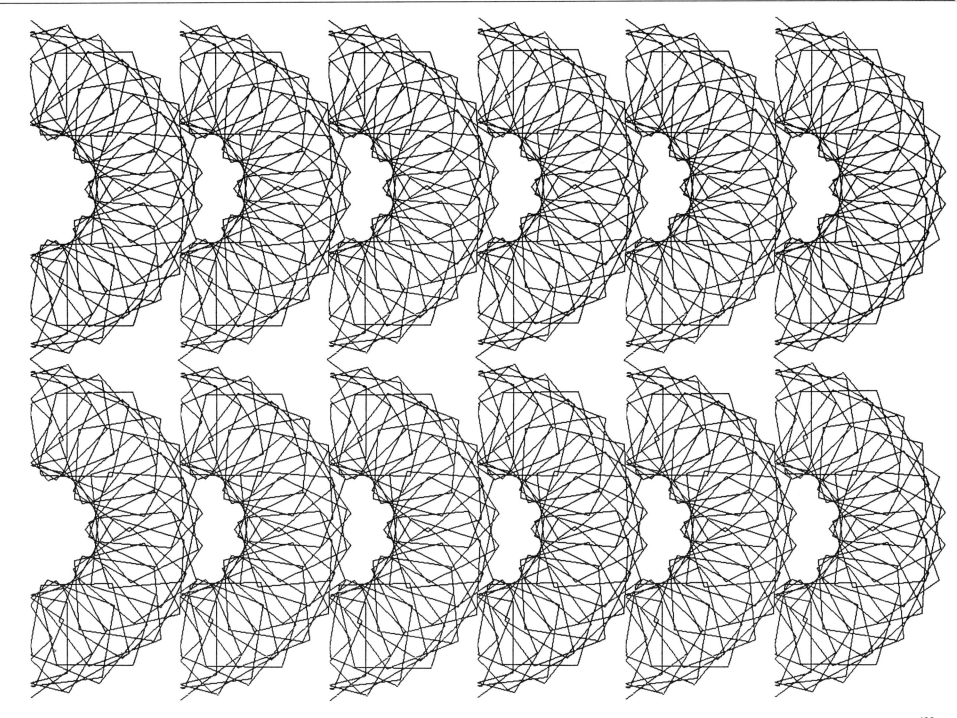

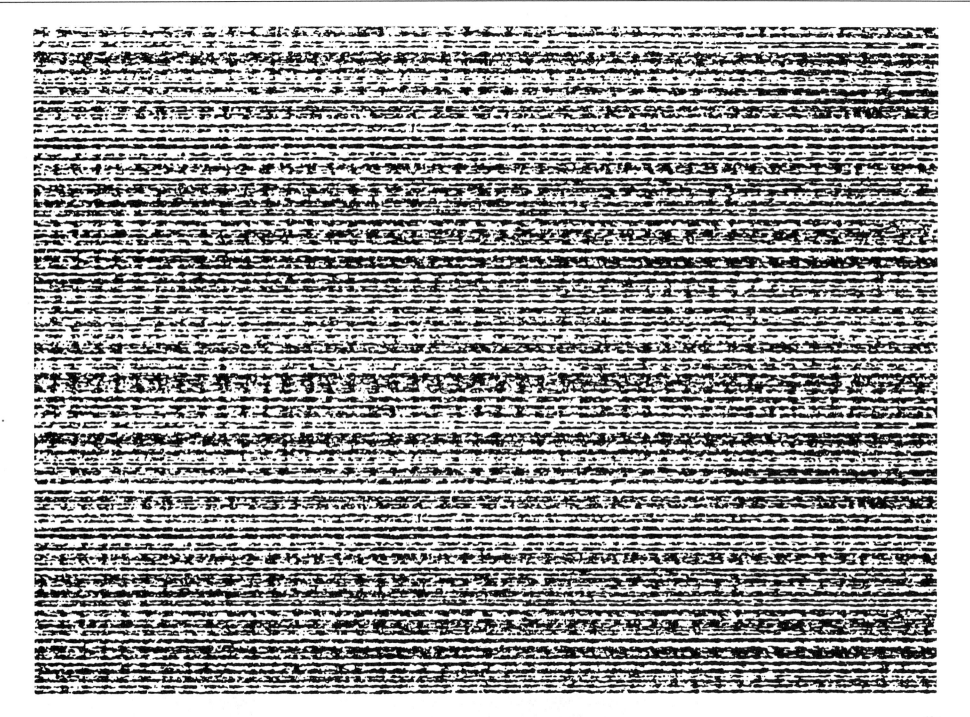

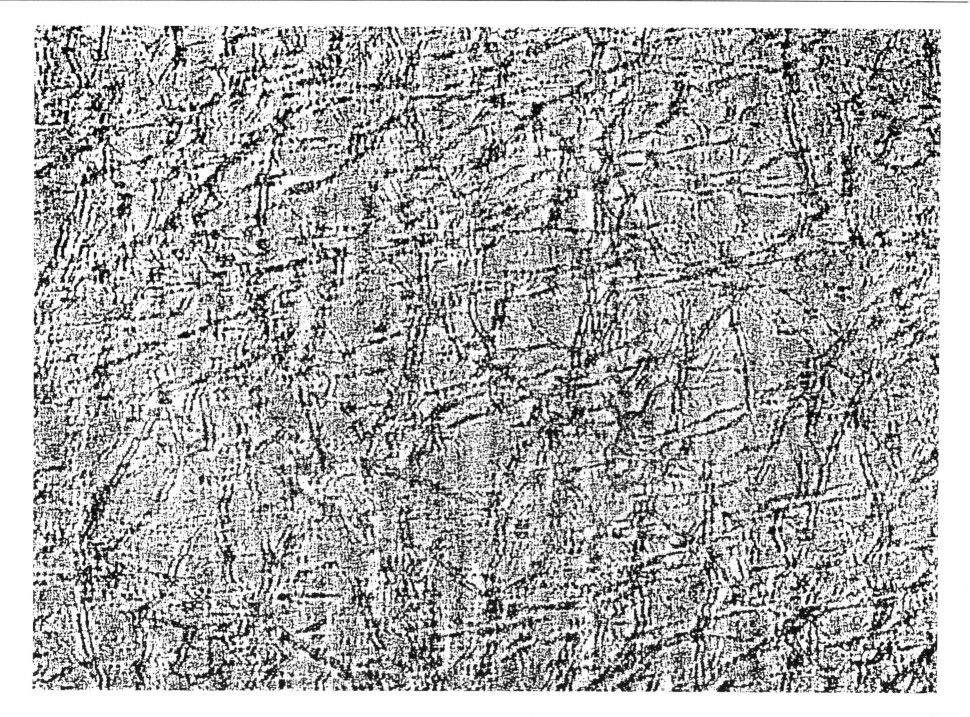

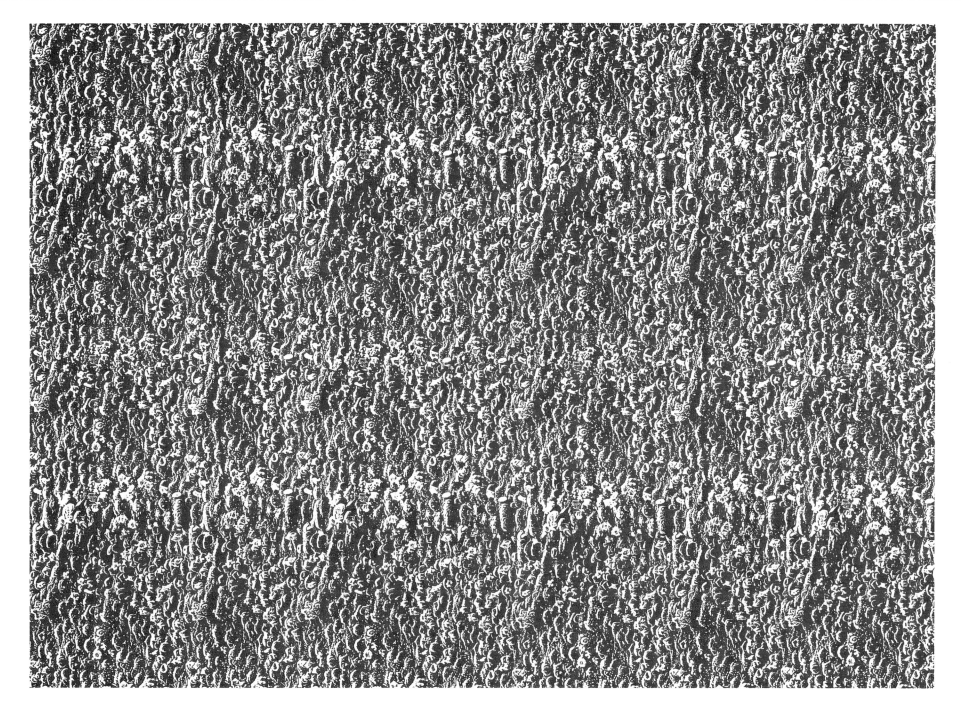

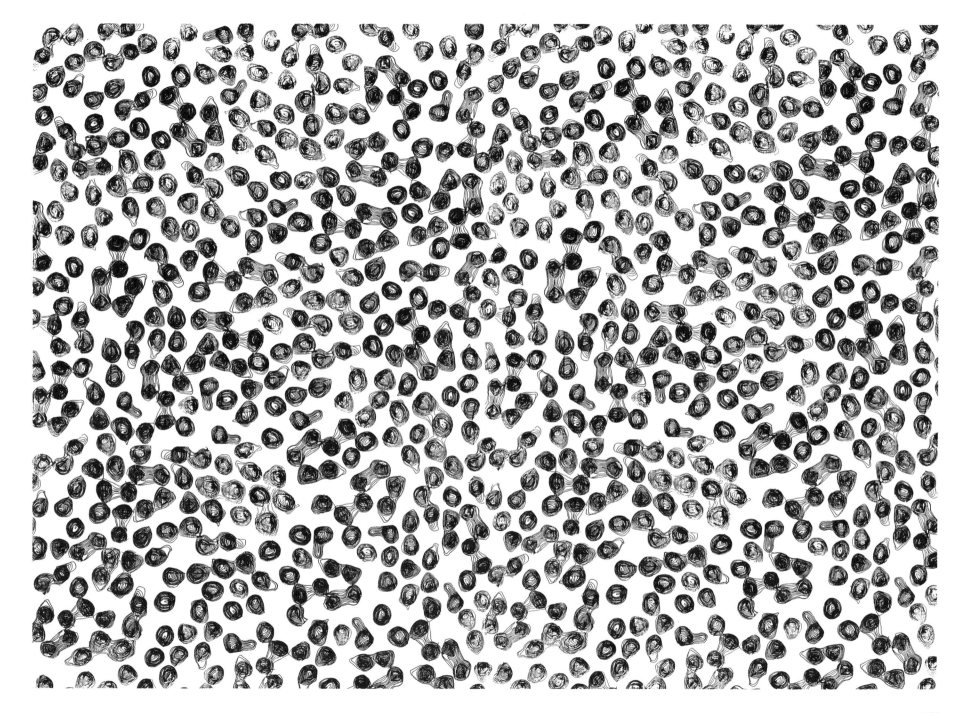

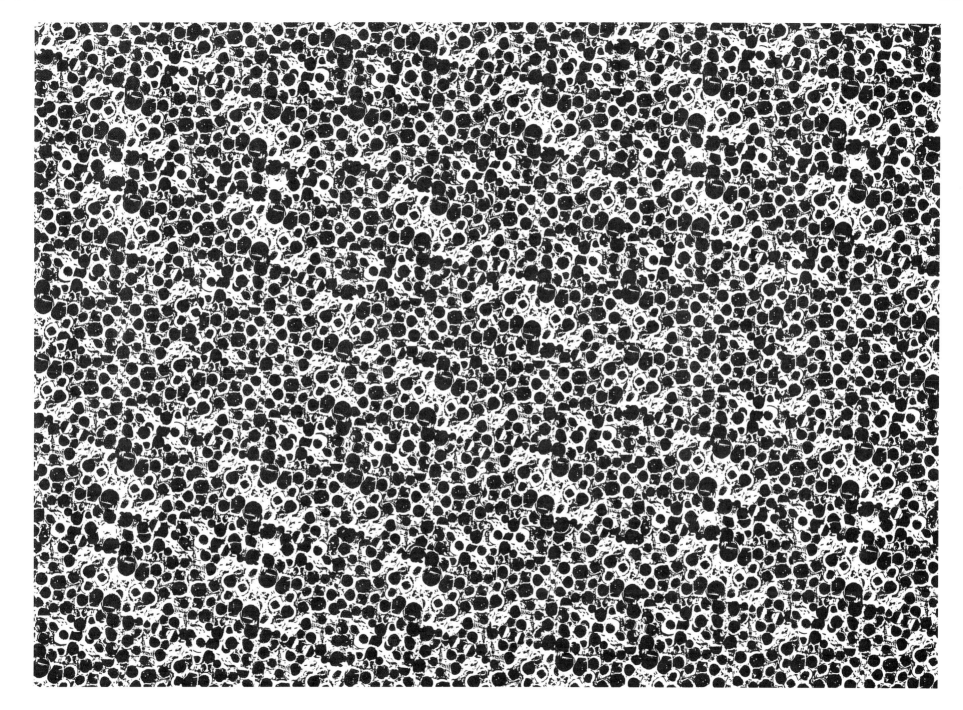

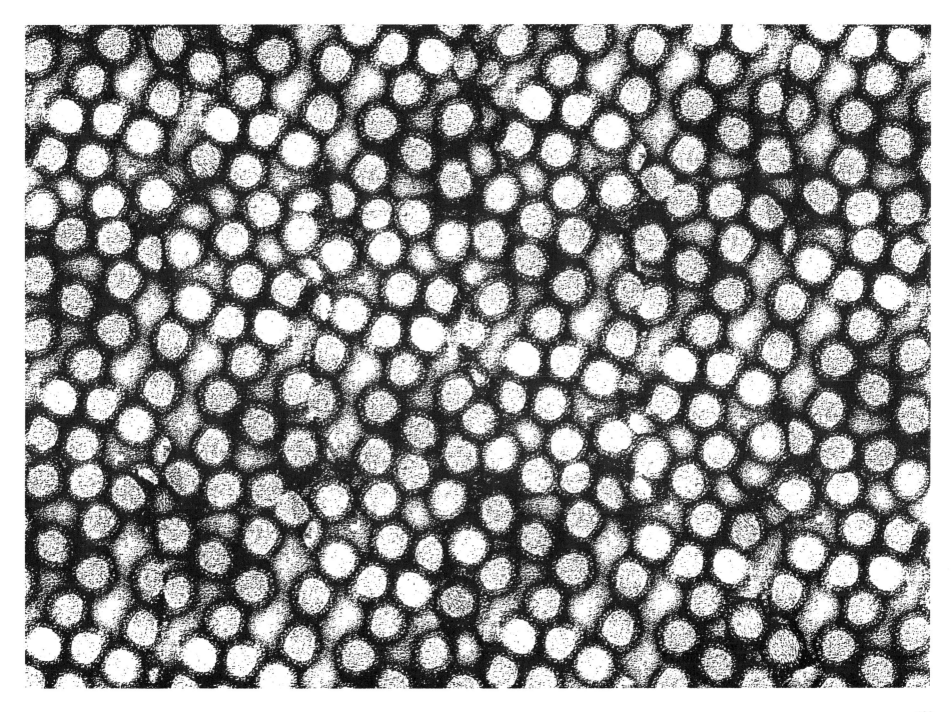

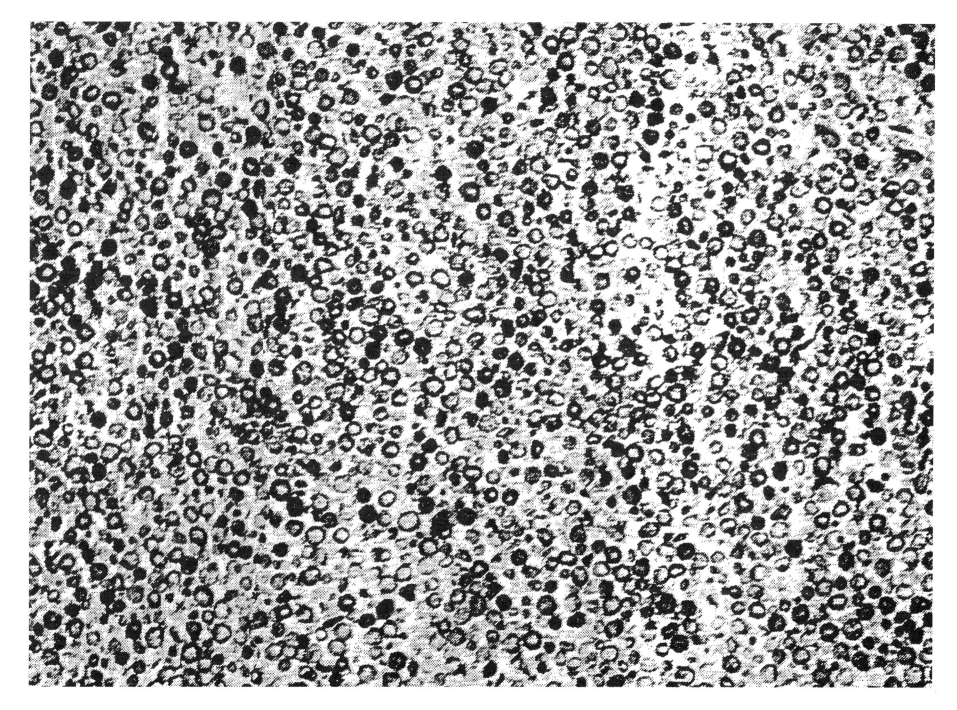

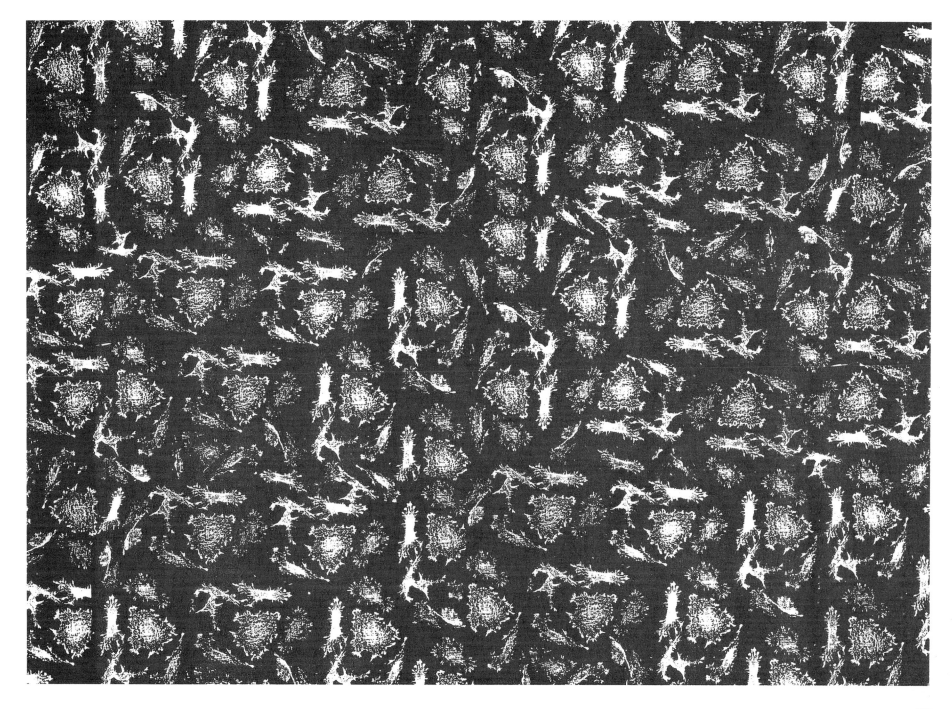

TYPE & COLOR: A HANDBOOK OF CREATIVE COMBINATIONS

Technological innovations in printing, computer graphics and desktop publishing systems have made the commercial arts environment considerably more competitive. Graphic artists must perform quickly, creatively and accurately. **Type & Color** enables graphics artists to spec type in color quickly and efficiently. The ten sheets of color typefaces printed on acetate overlays can be combined with the hundreds of color bars, making it possible to experiment with thousands of color/type combinations right at the drawing board. In minutes the eye will rapidly judge what the mind has conceived.

160 pages including 10 clear acetate overlays
$34.95   **ISBN 0-935603-19-0**
                              Hardcover

DESIGNS FOR MARKETING NO. 1 PRIMO ANGELI

Journey with this premiere graphic designer as he traces the development of his well-known commercial designs—including DHL, TreeSweet, Cambridge, Henry Weinhard beer, California Cooler—from initial client meetings to the finished designs. Packed with more than 300 four-color photographs and accompanied by lively text, this is an essential reference for graphic artists and marketers.

144 pages   **ISBN 0-935603-10-7**
$27.95   **Hardcover**

COLOR SOURCEBOOK I

Originally published with great success in Japan, **Color SourceBook I** is a treasure trove of ideas for creating color combinations, shapes and patterns. Color concepts under the headings 'Natural,' 'Oriental,' and 'High-Tech' provide interesting and useful color design combinations to help create an appropriate color framework for the designer to work within. Instructions are specific, geared toward the professional, yet clear enough to be useful to the student.

112 pages   **ISBN 0-935603-28-X**
$15.95   **Softcover**

COLOR SOURCEBOOK II

Today color and design go hand in hand, and for this reason **Color SourceBook II** is an indispensable tool for creating color combinations, shapes and patterns. This second essential volume furnishes the designer with color concepts under the headings 'Pop' 'Retro-Modern' and 'Post Modern,' and creates color and design fields for the designer to work within.

112 pages   **ISBN 0-935603-29**
$15.95   **Softcover**

COLOR HARMONY

A step-by-step guide to choosing and combing colors, **Color Harmony** includes 1,662 individual color combinations; dozens of full-color photos to show you how your color schemes will look; a four-color conversion chart; 61 full-size color charts and much more.

158 pages   **ISBN 0-935603-06-9**
$15.95   **Softcover**

THE GUILD 4

Since 1985, **The Guild** has served as the most prestigious juried showcase for American craft artists. Now in its fourth edition, **The Guild** presents the work of 400 leading artisans who work in ceramics, wood, stained glass, wrought iron, fibers, tapestry and a variety of other media. Their work is challenging, intriguing and highly varied in design and stylistic approach. The objects are faithfully reproduced in full color, with a minimum of one page devoted to each artist's work.

432 pages   **ISBN 0-935603-16-6**
$49.95   **Hardcover**

THE BEST IN MEDICAL ADVERTISING AND GRAPHICS

Four hundred stunning and remarkably ingenious medical ads and illustrations have been brought together in this book. This must-have reference captures, in full-color, the astonishing creativity of a group of graphic arts specialists whose work has never been seen in such entirety. **The Best in Medical Advertising and Graphics** not only displays the exceptional graphic techniques of the industries' top creative talents, but also presents the effort behind the ads. Included is information on advertising goals and strategies, design objectives, audience targeting and client's restrictions.

256 pages   **ISBN 0-935603-17-4**
$49.95   **Hardcover**

DESIGN IN PLASTICS

We are a world society pervaded by plastics. But plastics have not been a part of human history for long enough to have a well-established tradition of what exactly constitutes excellence of design in the new medium. **Design in Plastics** looks at design as a continuum of disciplines that combine to make a product look the way it does as an expression of the time in which it was created. Products cover the spectrum of what is available in the workplace, at home, at play and in between. Accompanying text highlights notable features and reasons for selection, along with designer, firm, material and client for each product.

256 pages   ISBN 0-953603-11-5
$49.95   Hardcover

BEST OF SCREEN PRINTING

This first major book devoted to the graphic rather than functional aspects of screen printing captures the elegance and utility of this important art form. The book contains superb screen print designs of limited edition art, garments, textiles, vinyl goods and posters, all reproduced in vibrant color. Each illustration is accompanied by information on design strategy, marketing and technical details.

256 pages   ISBN 0-935603-17-4
$49.95   Hardcover

VOLUME ONE: TRADEMARKS & SYMBOLS OF THE WORLD — THE ALPHABET IN DESIGN

This wonderful resource and idea book presents more than 1,700 contemporary designs from a variety of sources for every letter of the alphabet. An essential resource for anyone involved in typography, sign and logo design and creating corporate identities.

192 pages   ISBN 4-7601-0451-8
$24.95   Softcover

VOLUME TWO: TRADEMARKS & SYMBOLS OF THE WORLD — DESIGN ELEMENTS

If you design packages, ads, corporate logos, or signage, you must have this resource guide in your design library. It features more than 1,700 design elements that can add pizzazz to any printed piece.

192 pages   ISBN 4-7601-0450-X
$24.95   Softcover

VOLUME THREE: TRADEMARKS & SYMBOLS OF THE WORLD PICTOGRAM & SIGN DESIGN

This third volume in the **Trademarks & Symbols of the World** series includes pictogram and sign design from all over the world. An incredible variety of visual messages are available here: "no left turn," "camel crossing," "volcanic activity," "I love you" and 1796 more.

232 pages   ISBN 0-935603-30-1
$24.95   Softcover

THE BEST OF AD CAMPAIGNS!

Presents 30 of the best recent advertising campaigns as selected by the American Association of Advertising Agencies. Up to twelve pages are devoted to each campaign, and they include every subject, from business-to-business to fast food, and services to durable goods.

256 pages   ISBN 0-935603-09-3
$49.95   Hardcover

LETTERHEAD DESIGNS 1

Letterheads, Corporate Identity Programs and Brand & Service Marks

A recognizable and effective visual identity is a necessity for businesses of all sizes and types, from makers of consumer goods to restaurants and retail stores. Here is a comprehensive selection of the most exciting and effective current designs for corporate identity packages, including letterheads, business cards, envelopes, stationery supplies, logotypes and much more.

256 pages   ISBN: 0-935603-37-9
$49.95   Hardcover
Available   June 1990

THE BEST NEW U.S. & INTERNATIONAL LABEL DESIGNS: 2

Label Designs 2 is an essential sourcebook for label and packaging designers, graphic artists and marketing and advertising professionals. It is both an index to current trends and an inspiration for new and effective work. No business, no designer, no advertising agency can afford to be without this indispensable collection.

256 pages   ISBN 0-935603-31-X
$49.95   Hardcover